RICH ON PAPER
POOR ON LIFE

3 Paths to More Meaning (and Money)

Philip McKernan

BRAVEHEART
MEDIA

Writing Support: Zander Robertson & Joy Gregory
Designed by Matthew Lütz
Proofread by Alvin Nirenberg & Janet Galligan

To the most generous human I have ever met.
To the most intuitive women I have ever encountered.
To my friend whose belief is unwavering.
To my mother.

I love you.

CONTENTS

FOREWORD

PhD, Clinical Psychologist

I've read hundreds of psychological and personal growth books over the years representing most all of the masters in the field. This book you hold in your hands is by far the most important and poignantly significant. So much so, that I find it hard to put into words how grateful I am to have met Philip McKernan, and the task of introducing his abilities and this book leaves me a bit speechless. Philip's work is all about "connection," which is what gives life meaning, what all human beings desperately crave, and the single most important thing that underscores happiness and well-being. We inhabit a world and culture that promote disconnection from self, others, and the environment at every turn. Caught in the throes of constant technological intrusions, over-extended schedules, and comparison-based striving, I can think of nothing more important than learning how to turn back the tide of modern life and repair these vital connections.

Philip is an extraordinarily gifted life-coach who guides people in their instinctive drive to be more authentically "connected" to themselves, others, and a life purpose. His methods emphasize experiential and vicarious learning, which are the most powerful forms of education, and which enable immediate internal shifts that tend to expand over time. He teaches people how to get out of their heads and into their hearts, where real knowing and change occurs. Most importantly, he leads by example, and is one of the most truly authentic human beings in the personal growth field. His exceedingly grounded, humble and personal approach provides a safe environment for undertaking this kind of work, and asking yourself the difficult questions that need to be asked.

The first time I observed Philip deliver a talk onstage, I was spellbound by the raw, vulnerable honesty of his delivery and the utterly profound, yet basic truths he shares. He takes you straight to the core of what your heart is yearning for, and I recognized instantly that his messages could elevate the quality of my life to unimaginable levels. I was not alone in my perspective. After three full days of listening to many other world renowned speakers, Philip's presentation was the one that everyone was still talking about, and that left us all with a palpable excitement about what is possible for us in this life.

Since that first talk, I've had the privilege and opportunity to attend weekend workshops with Philip as well as his sacred Irish retreat, a pilgrimage back to his homeland. Although I was excited for my first weekend workshop with him, I was unprepared for it to be the single most transformative experience I have had. Philip and the attendees inspired me to really take stock of my life, and uncover some of my biggest fears and fiercest longings. After acknowledging those truths and experiencing the utter clarity that ensues, it was impossible to go back to old ways of being. That weekend marked a very clear turning point in my personal life history, where I can look back and see a dramatic difference in the before and after. Since that experience, my parenting embarked on a journey of greater engagement and connection, and I found myself much more honest and vulnerable in my other relationships. I have been able to let go of the things that don't serve me, and – perhaps most importantly – I have learned to hear, listen to and trust my gut, which always knows the answer.

In his book and workshops, Philip discusses and answers many of the most important yet most elusive questions of life. Who am I really? How do I grow my sense of self-worth? Am I doing the work I was meant to do? Am I in the right relationship? Am I living where I most want to live? What is my greater purpose on this earth? What do I love doing so much that I would pay to do it? With every subject he tackles, he gets straight to the root of the issue and focuses on the simple, unarguable truths of the matter. He demonstrates through teaching and example how finding your voice and speaking your truth leads to trusting yourself and real clarity. These tools enable you to live in a way that is aligned with your highest principles, and remind us that "if wealth is to be sought, it must be sought as a healthy byproduct of a life well-lived. This kind of integrated approach to work, self, relationships, brings the greatest ease, possibility and contentment that can be known."

Until now, the magic that occurs through Philip's teachings has been a well kept secret shared only among the devotees who have been transformed by his workshops and coaching. For the first time, these important messages and inspiring examples from real people have been beautifully captured and conveyed in this powerful book.

In "Rich on Paper, Poor on Life: three paths to more meaning (and money)", Philip convinces us that the heart longs for simplicity, passion, love and meaning. The passion, he says, is there all along, it's just a matter of coming back to one's self in order to find it. He reminds us that the heart of every individual longs for the same thing: to love and be loved.

This book illuminates not just Philip's transformative messages and the poignant journeys of others, but also the man behind these powerful truths. Philip's own personal transparency invites and inspires others to match his level of candor and self-reflection. From the perspective of being a client, as well as a clinical psychologist immersed in the positive psychology/human potential movement, I've never encountered a leader in this arena who is more gifted at conveying so powerfully, yet so simply, what matters most in this life.

If you have ever wondered how to create a life full of meaning, authenticity and passion, you are human – and Philip's book is for you.

PROLOGUE:

FINDING MY VOICE

"We are all born leaders, but we don't all believe that."
~ Philip McKernan

When I write the book of my own life, I may title it, *No Thank You, Mr. President.* The background story behind that title highlights one of the many defining moments from my youth.

As with many life events, I only began to make sense of the story's real importance years after it happened. I share it here because I believe many people have had similar experiences in that we only come to understand life events long after they occur. Indeed, the idea that the "past is prologue" in that it informs who we are today, is a central theme of my work as a coach and mentor.

The story goes back to a place I spent much of my youth, at the Newlands Golf Club (near Dublin) where my dad was a member. One day the club received some grand news: the President of Ireland, Mr. Patrick Hillery, was going to be golfing at the club.

The club was honoured by the visit and started making arrangements. Since my father was a respected member of the club, he was asked if one of his sons could caddy for the president.

Those unfamiliar with golf often misunderstand a caddy's role. Most think a caddy carries the clubs. What they don't realize is that a real caddy also advises the golfer on all aspects of the game. This includes shot selection, club selection, and telling him about the physical characteristics of the course.

When asked, my father said yes. I'm not sure why I was chosen, but at age of about 12, I found myself caddying for the President of Ireland. I knew the course well, but a lack of belief in myself led me to keep my mouth shut when I should have been advising him. I found it painful to watch the president make poor choice after poor choice. But still, I said nothing.

The major issue was his club selection. He was having a hard time judging the distance to each hole, mostly because the course was hilly. I watched silently, but was bothered by his poor choices. In my mind, I predicted every shot he made. Being so familiar with the terrain, I knew when he was going to hit the bunker, when he was going to go over the back of the green, and when he was going to hit the trees. I knew he was misreading the course.

On the fifteenth hole, President Hillery pulled out his eight iron for his second shot. If executed well, he thought that shot would put him on the green. I knew better, and couldn't be quiet any longer. "You want to use a seven iron on this shot," I blurted. The president stopped in his tracks, and looked up at me with a surprised face.

He replied, "I should use the seven iron?" I said, "Yeah, it's all uphill and it's a lot further than it looks from this angle." The president said, "Alright, seven iron it is then."

Try to picture the scene: the President of Ireland was just told by a pre-pubescent 12-year-old boy that he couldn't hit an eight iron as far as he thought he could. The time that passed between when I offered my advice, and when he finally took his shot, was the longest 30 to 60 seconds of my life. I started doubting my own advice, and even regretted opening my mouth.

My thoughts were, "What if I'm wrong? What if he hits it long? I'm going to look like a fool." I was mortified! The President stepped up to the ball and took his swing. The moment he connected with the ball, I knew he'd made perfect contact. Now it was down to the right club selection.

The ball was well hit, and on the right line. We'd soon know whether I'd selected the right club. I held my breath as the ball landed just short of the hole, then ran up to a pin high position within 10 feet. We were both thrilled with his shot. He looked over at me and said, "Where the hell have you been all day?"

Over the final three holes, the President wanted my opinion on each shot. Since I knew the course so well, I provided him with insight into club selection, and how he should set up his shots. The truth is, he played like crap all day, so I can't say I turned it around for him. But I couldn't have made it any worse by speaking up, and in fact, I know my advice helped him.

At the end of the round, the President tipped me £50—an enormous sum for a boy that age. My Dad had warned me against taking any money. He told me I should just be grateful for having the honour of caddying for the President.

To hell with that! I was 12 years old and needed some toys! Because the President didn't carry cash, his security man handed me the money. As we approached the clubhouse, the President turned to me and asked, "Would you join me for lunch?"

I responded, "No thank you Mr. President, my Mom is waiting in the parking lot."

When I got in the car with my Mom, she peppered me with questions about the President. "What was he like? Was he kind? Was he a good golfer? Did he swear? Did he smoke cigars?" She wanted to know everything. I told her that he was a nice man, and that he'd paid me well. When we were on the motorway, I told her, "oh yeah, and he asked me to have lunch with him."

"What?" she asked.

I explained that I told him I had to go because my Mom was in the parking lot. I'll never forget the look on my Mom's face as she nearly had a conniption fit! All the way home, she muttered under her breath, "Only my son would turn down the President for lunch. Only my son . . ."

I've told the story several times over the years. It's simple, cute, and has a funny ending thanks to my flustered Mom's reaction and muttering. But it wasn't until the past few years that I began to understand this story in a new light. I still love the personal aspects of the story. But having watched so many clients find their own voices, I now see it as a story in my own process to find my voice.

So many people struggle with this issue every day. It's as though there's a little voice inside us repeating, "why would anyone want to hear what you have to say? What right do you have to speak up?'"

This little voice is self-sabotage. There's no way I could do what I do if I believed that nagging little voice. Don't get me wrong, I still hear that voice every now and then, but it's not as strong as it once was. I suspect it will continue to weaken with time.

The day I caddied for President Hillery, that voice was dominant. It was so dominant that I kept my mouth shut for 14 holes of golf—even though I knew my advice might help the president.

You might be thinking, "Philip, you were only 12 years old, it's natural that you'd be a bit intimidated by the President." I agree to an extent, and if it was only children who bit their tongue for fear of looking stupid, then I probably wouldn't be telling this story right now. But you and I both know that's not the case.

Many (if not most) people keep their truth inside for fear of looking stupid or because they believe they have nothing to add. How many people have a hidden desire to write, sing, paint, get involved in politics, or start a business? How many of them don't get involved because they don't believe they're good enough? I believe the majority of people feel this way. They won't speak up or act up as long as they place a low value upon themselves.

OUR BIGGEST FEAR: THE TRUTH

Finding one's voice is a process that takes time. Life can beat us down. Many of us endure years of being told we shouldn't believe in ourselves. After that, finding our voice is scary for entirely different reasons. While many of us have been told that what we're really afraid of is public speaking, I say bullshit. A fear of speaking in front of others is not our greatest common fear. Our greatest common fear is that we don't believe that what we have to say matters. In this way, the fear of public speaking stems from a fear of not being loved.

Let me repeat: when we say we're scared of public speaking, what we're really saying is that we are scared of making a mistake, of being judged. Deep down, we're afraid of not being loved.

For many of us, speaking publically about topics that matter to us is the most vulnerable we can get. It's one big opportunity to be honest—and find ourselves feeling unloved in return. Because of this fear, I believe many public speakers don't speak from the heart. They're simply too scared to let people see the reality. They believe that if they speak with their own voice, they won't be loved.

Over the years, I've had several opportunities to speak unauthentically. I admit there've been times I've done exactly that. But it wasn't until I started speaking vulnerably that I felt fulfillment from speaking. That's because there's enormous power in finding one's voice, and in speaking that voice. The fear we feel is a good indicator that we're on the right path. In spite of the fact that we fear we won't be loved, speaking our truth is one of the most important things we can do to put ourselves on the path towards authentic love.

This book is all about the transformative power that comes when we learn to speak with our own voice. It changes your life; it changes the lives of those around you. Speaking the truth gives yourself—and others—access to a truth that wasn't formerly expressed, but needed to be said. (Just ask the former President of Ireland.)

The voice I speak of, is our intuition.

WHO AM I REALLY

Am I really the person I see in the mirror whose face is wrinkled and worn?

Or is there something I don't see in this one-dimensional window?

Am I really the work I do or the house I live in?

Or is there something I have not yet met within myself?

Am I really the husband I am told I am?

Or the voice I hear echo back at me when I speak to others?

Am I really the person others see when they look at me?

Or are they seeing a person through a set of eyes they themselves do not know?

What if there is someone within me that I have yet to meet who is better looking than I am, smarter than I believe I am, and more famous than I could ever be?

Would you like to meet him?

~ Philip McKernan

INTRODUCTION

"Success in manufactured in the mind
while happiness is cultivated in the soul."
~ Philip McKernan

THE INSPIRATION: UNMASKING THE CELTIC TIGER

Anyone who's heard me speak will know that I am Irish. It should come as no surprise, then, that this book's roots stretch back to my own in Ireland and are based on my business and life experience. In fact, the concept of writing a book like, Rich on Paper, Poor on Life, started during the heady years of the Celtic Tiger.

Looking back, I can even pinpoint the specific event. It was 1994 and the opening game of the World Cup of Football (soccer) was being played at Giant Stadium in East Rutherford, New Jersey. The mighty Italians, then three-time World Cup champions, were playing the lowly Irish.

It is no overstatement to say that football is akin to religion in Italy. It's the country's most popular sport and all would undoubtedly cite football as their number one sport. That's not the case in Ireland, where football is the third most popular sport, falling after Hurling and Gaelic Football. Ireland's population is 4.5 million and few would argue with the suggestion that its 1994

World Cup team was a ragtag squad of scrappers. The Irish had never won the World Cup. In fact, the Irish rarely even qualified for the tournament. Needless to say, the odds were heavily stacked in the Italian's favour.

Still, the Irish came to play that day, and they battled for every ball. Clearly the underdogs, they played with a spirit that belied what some would have written off as an obvious lack of skill. To make a long story short, Ireland's dogged determination won the game.

But let me take a minute to set the stage. Even before the game started, the atmosphere was electric. Seventy-thousand fans were crammed into every corner of the stadium, singing and chanting their teams' songs. The Italian fans were optimistic—and likely a little bit cocky. The Irish fans were just glad to be there. With Irish World Cup appearances a rarity, these fans were determined to make the most of the occasion. After a time, the game settled into a rhythm, with the Italians making flourishing attacks and the Irish scrapping for every ball. It was vintage underdog football, and the Irish weren't going without a fight.

In the eleventh minute, a competent but unspectacular midfielder named Ray Houghton found himself with a little room as the ball travelled through the air towards him. Normally the kind of player who would advance the team forward with proficient passes, Ray didn't merit the attention of a star player or goal scorer.

But when the ball hit his chest on that day, Ray was transformed. Nobody, least of all the Italian players, expected him to make a superstar-like strike. But that moment was different. Right after picking up the loose ball during the game against the Italians, Ray drew his leg back and blasted the ball towards the goal.

While fans and teammates wondered what was happening, the ball soared over the head of the giant Italian goalkeeper. Ray was 35 yards from the goal line—and the ball was in the net.

The hearts of Irish fans, including 35,000 at the game and millions more around the world, skipped a collective beat as the ball rocketed into the goal. Houghton the grinder hadn't just scored the biggest goal of his life, he'd scored one of the biggest goals in Irish football history.

From that goal on, the scrappy Irish held their ground. Playing like they belonged on that World-class pitch, they maintained a hard-fought 1-0 victory over the mighty Italians. The entire nation of Ireland was overcome with jubilation.

Looking back, I believe the implications of that goal went far beyond a football victory. While the seeds of the economic powerhouse that would be known as the Celtic Tiger had already been sown, Houghton's goal was like emotional fertilizer for a financial boom ignited by a series of fortunate events.

Inspired by the goal, and a win over the Italian team the people of Ireland rode an economic wave of national pride expressed in economic confidence. What made that win even more impressive was the fact that the Italians got to the World Cup final and were narrowly beaten by the Brazilians. The game finished 0:0 and the final was decided on penalties for the first time in history.

Before the Celtic Tiger, Ireland was relatively poor compared to its European neighbours. Fifteen years after the advent of the Celtic Tiger, the nation became the second-wealthiest nation on Earth per capita, a vast improvement from its initial ranking as the second-poorest in Europe. As with most proud Irishmen and Irishwomen, I vividly remember the feeling of the era. The Celtic Tiger heralded a new collective awareness of what it meant to be Irish. As a young entrepreneur at the time, I recognized my home country as a kind of Promised Land. For me and many of my compatriots, it was like we'd died in one country and gone to heaven in another.

People in the business community saw the Celtic Tiger as proof of our worth. Ireland finally had a seat at the table of economic power, and the sense that we'd earned our place helped us develop a certain confidence we'd previously lacked.

To me, Ray Houghton's goal, and the Irish win over the mighty Italians, was the benchmark moment of that newfound Irish confidence. It was like Houghton helped us believe that we could put up the good fight—and that we deserved to win. Behind that single football victory, however, is a more complicated truth. In reality, the global high-tech sector sparked Ireland's economic boom. Due to a mix of factors, computer companies (notably Dell) began locating major offices in Ireland. Encouraged by major tax incentives offered by a government hell-bent on economic expansion, high-tech firms found it easy to set up shop in Ireland.

While the high-tech sector started the party, it wasn't long before the secondary industries showed up. Luxury products and car sales exploded. And that was just the beginning. The growth in other industries paled in comparison to the unprecedented boom in the construction industry.

Ireland, an ancient country with a medieval infrastructure that also shaped its economic mindset, was suddenly busy. There were more cars on the old roads, more houses being built (everywhere!) and more offices and commercial spaces under construction. In step with what many countries do when experiencing a boom,

Ireland's government and banks stepped in with even more economic stimuli.

As part of that equation, lending standards were lowered as the banks rushed in to finance building projects and consumer spending. People who used to save their money now borrowed money to buy second homes, second cars, motorcycles, boats and other consumer goods. Convinced the economic boom could not end, they used the equity in their home or other properties as collateral to finance new purchases.

When the end came, it was catastrophic. The Celtic Tiger crashed and burned during the global financial crisis of 2007. While there's no doubt that corresponding economic crises in other parts of the world played a major role in ending the party, it also would be irresponsible to suggest there weren't warning signs within Ireland herself.

Let me be more specific. The global financial crisis wouldn't have affected Ireland nearly as bad if the Irish people weren't behaving so irresponsibly with their personal and public finances, myself included. Looking back, there were numerous signs that the economy was not sustainable, and numerous opportunities to give the economy a break by slowing down the lending were ignored.

The opposite happened. When minor economic slowdowns occurred, the politicians brought in new rounds of stimulus programs. Reacting to private interests, they lowered lending standards and dropped interest rates to ramp-up the economic engine now known globally as the Celtic Tiger.

It was the economic equivalent of feeding sugar and caffeine to an overstimulated, diabetic and addicted nation. Every time we got more, we wanted more. Consumption begot more consumption. It was like our hands were in the clouds searching for more money while our heads were in sand hiding from fundamental truths about the difference between More and Enough.

No longer the svelte creature of that victorious World Cup game, the Celtic Tiger quickly warped into a fat exotic zoo cat on life support. And the metaphor of a fat cat paints more than a symbolic picture. By the time the big crash came along and killed the mighty tiger, the Irish boom had contributed to a host of physical and mental health problems related to obesity.

Interestingly enough, the eventual collapse of the Irish economy was not a surprise. Many knew the Tiger was struggling and that's why several successive governments continued to feed this once mighty beast—even after it was obvious the food being offered could never be enough.

When all is said and done, however, it is too simplistic to blame Irish governments or banks. It's also too easy to blame the global financial crisis; too easy because those efforts to assign blame ignore the one simple truth that whispers in the ears of Irish people. The whisper says: "You did this to yourself." And like it or not, it's true.

The bottom line is that nobody was ever marched into a bank at gunpoint and forced to sign a mortgage document for a second or third home. Nor was anyone's family ever taken ransom with the purchase of a boat as condition for their release. The people of Ireland had other options. In the end, we screwed ourselves by over consuming, and by forgetting the things that make life worth living. Individuals were ignoring their own truths. Individuals had lost our own voices.

In sum, we got greedy. We forgot what was important. We chose gadgets over happiness, fancy over fulfillment. The global financial crisis would have had dire consequences for Ireland. But without the massive debt of its citizens, its impact would have been dramatically less devastating. People failed themselves.

Many chose to be rich on paper but poor on life. Some lost the very knick-knacks they thought they needed. Others lost family homes, committed suicide, got divorced, found themselves estranged from family and friends, or became ill. All too many survived physically, but were left barely able to cope with the combined mental stress of fear and guilt.

> *"A man who doesn't have peace of mind has no mind at all."*
> *~ Philip McKernan*

GETTING LOST IN THE CELTIC TIGER

Not everyone got sucked into the vortex, though. I recall one story that stands out. In the midst of the Celtic Tiger, my brother-in-law was building a beautiful little cottage on the West Coast of Ireland. I remember when he proudly explained how he paid for the cottage with cash rather than a mortgage, as was the practice at the time.

I thought he was nuts, and I let him know it. Seeing myself as a bit of a hot shot, I explained to him the principle of leverage and tried to impress upon him how much further his money could have stretched had he used one asset to mortgage another. Had he only been smarter, he could have bought several properties by leveraging the cash he had. To my dismay, he ignored my advice, choosing instead to forego the power of leverage and build the cottage with cash over a period of a few years.

In fairness, mine was the prevailing mindset of the time. The essence of that mindset was simple: because one can buy more, one should buy more. I bought into it as millions of others did. More, more, more. That was the mantra of the Celtic Tiger era.

At the time that I got caught up in this mindset, I was young and, alongside my older brother, was busy building a successful business in the coffee industry. Convinced of the wisdom of leverage, I took the money I was earning in coffee and started investing in real estate. (The relaxed lending standards of the day certainly helped!)

Looking back, I was one of the lucky ones. I managed to escape the worst of the financial carnage. What I didn't escape was the loss of my peace of mind. In the pursuit of money and growth for growth's sake, I did what most of my countrywomen and men did; I ignored passion and happiness in my own life and pursued wealth with the naive assumption that happiness followed achievement. (And take note of that sentence because the implication is that achievement is prerequisite of happiness is common—and dead wrong.)

Today, my brother-in-law owns a stunning cottage on the West Coast of Ireland—free and clear as he started. While many of the sophisticated investors preaching leverage and growth during the boom lost their properties, my brother-in-law's property was never in financial jeopardy. More importantly, he has more than a physical sanctuary. He has peace of mind. For as long as he lives, he'll never have to live in fear of losing the haven he built and paid for without worrying about what that property might "do" for other investments. By choosing peace-of-mind over growth for growth's sake, he's been richly rewarded.

With hindsight, I believe his choice of happiness over achievement allowed him to realize—and live—his authentic dream. In hindsight, I should have taken counsel from him!

USING INTUITION TO FIND MY WAY OUT

Please don't be fooled into thinking this was an Irish Problem. It's a modern-day epidemic affecting millions (and likely billions) around the world. Irish people are not stupid. On the contrary, they are resilient and street-wise people who unconsciously fell victim to the kind of mass peer pressure that camouflaged how their own lack of awareness put them at risk.

Intuitively, I eventually understood that something was wrong with the prevailing pattern. But Celtic Tiger-era Ireland was no place for intuition. Even though I was pretty sure something was wrong, I was surrounded by people who were borrowing money to make money—and my emerging viewpoint was shared by very few.

That experience with the Celtic Tiger has influenced the work I do now more than anything else. Seeing it happen first hand helped me realize the real cost of putting achievement over happiness is social versus economic. You lose money, sure. But your real losses are incalculable. It was the greatest economic party Ireland has ever seen and its people were left with what I call a Social Invoice. It's a bill many will pay for the rest of their lives. It's also a bill that insight could have helped many avoid completely.

Economies will rise and fall. Most people in most of the developed world have the wealth, ability, and the opportunity to live fulfilling lives that include peace of mind. The Celtic Tiger experience taught me that lack of money isn't the problem. The real issues are rooted in a widespread lack of self-worth, trust, intuition and vision. Living rich on paper but poor on life is an epidemic that expands far beyond the shores of Ireland. Over time, I made it my intention to warn against future Celtic Tigers from happening. I may not be able to single-handedly stop repeats of the Celtic Tiger, but if I can do anything about it, I must.

What I can do is work with individuals, one at a time or in small groups, to mitigate some of the damage and, where possible, to help people understand that more is no recipe for peace of mind. I cannot stop the boom-and-bust cycle of macroeconomics, but I can help to reduce the Social Invoice. I can help others out of the cycle of being rich on paper but poor on life.

To be clear, I'm not against financial wealth. What I'm against is sacrificing peace of mind for wealth. If wealth is to be sought, it must be sought as a healthy byproduct of a life well-lived. Too many people pay nothing more than lip service to well-being in favour of wealth building. Instead of seeking happiness now, they believe in happiness when.

But wealth and peace of mind don't have to be in opposition. Understanding how they can work in tandem begins with understanding that there is a cost to every action we take. As you'll see through the stories I share in this book, poor health is the price of eating unhealthy food, and poor relationships are the price of failing to love and cherish our spouses (and ourselves). Seeking riches at the expense of well-being exacts an immense cost to the spirit of every individual who tries it. You simply can't put well-being on the back-burner and expect to be well.

This book also addresses the notion that many of us believe there's something wrong with us. We feel broken. We look at the rich and famous and think, "if only my life was like theirs."

Very few look within. We assume the problem can be solved with more money, more cars, more stuff. The fundamental fallacy of that approach is that it leads people to believe, against evidence to the contrary, that achieving a greater level of wealth will make us better, fix our lives, and make us happier.

FIND YOUR VOICE, LIVE WITH PASSION

In my business, I have the pleasure and honour of working with remarkable people every day. My clients are often big vision people. Many have already accomplished much by the time they begin working with me. They typically have several more big goals they want to see through to fruition.

However, their deepest and most heartfelt goals almost always include some combination of the following:

1. Family (spending more time with kids or parents)
2. Spirituality (feeling a greater connection)
3. Contribution (giving back time or money)

When you analyze peoples' most heartfelt goals, you can see that each of them is also about relationships, be they with family, the true self or with others. Time and time again, I see that relationships are at the core of what my clients seek. That's why my work focuses on relationships. More precisely, I help my clients focus on their relationships to the key elements of their lives. This strategy is based on the knowledge that every person's personal path to well-being is through improved relationships, whether it be a relationship with one's self, with others or with the work we do.

Unfortunately, I often hear about these core desires expressed along with a belief that they are connected to massive wealth. That's because people think they need millions of dollars to achieve what they "really" want. This belief is counterproductive to the pursuit of what I call Real Wealth. Indeed, the pursuit of real wealth requires one let go of the notion that money buys happiness. This inner conflict can be stated more simply: it's a battle between the goals and aspirations of the head and the heart. The head is where we think we want something. The heart is where we know we need something.

CONFUSING PASSION

After discussing what my clients want at their core, we often move on and discuss the various areas of their life. One of the biggest topics that requires discussion is the world of work. This is where a conflicting pattern often emerges.

A very good number of my clients will explain to me how their job or business is their passion. It's this experience that's led me to believe passion is a misunderstood concept.

I say this because the same people who tell me that their job or business is their passion will, in the next breath, tell me they're going to quit their job or business the moment they make enough money so that they can do something else. Interestingly enough, the "something else" almost always involves relationships linked to one of the three heartfelt goals noted previously. What many people don't acknowledge is the disconnect.

To be clear, a passion is something you'd do for free if you had to, it's something you'd like to do for the rest of your life, no matter what. Indeed, a passion might cost you money rather than make you money. But why do so many people want to quit their job or business if it's their passion?

The answer is simple: they're not passionate about their job or business after all. In fact, most people don't know what they're passionate about. They can identify the things they really want (family time, contribution, experiences, spirituality), but not their passion. This leads people to try to turn their work into their passion. What they're really doing is hoping that one day they'll have enough money to do what they love. Effectively, this removes passion from their present, placing it in the always-distant future.

I start to see a shift in my clients when they bring those things that they love to the forefront of their thoughts and actions. This is the process of becoming rich on life instead of just rich on paper.

I'm not talking about taking a vow of poverty. On the contrary, when people undertake the journey of becoming rich in life, they ultimately find that material wealth follows. But rather than coming at the expense of well-being, wealth follows well-being.

The more in-touch my clients get with what's really important, the more they throw off the "get rich at all costs" mentality, the more they get rich on life. It's empowering for people to understand that living life comes first and material wealth follows behind to support the living. Too many people believe the opposite—that seeking well-being and happiness first is a recipe for poverty.

This is simply not true. In my work, I see many people chasing money in the false assumption that they'll be free to explore the good life they truly desire once they're financially fee. Good luck with that. It simply doesn't work. The rich on paper, poor on life mindset steals simplicity, passion, love, and meaning from the lives of millions daily.

I'm a big believer in looking within for answers to life's difficulties. Anyone who looks within will find that their heart longs for simplicity, passion, love and meaning.

To some of you, this may sound fluffy. But at least acknowledge that it's also true. People on their deathbeds do not lament the fact they didn't make certain investments or work a few more hours per week. But many people do regret not living their passion. They regret not practicing their art, spending time with their family or helping others more.

We long for simplicity, passion, love, and meaning—and then ignore those longings. Many people think they will find passion, love and meaning only after they generate a certain amount of money or wealth. But that behaviour comes at a cost. If this book gets you to stop and ask better questions, then you will be better off than the many millions of people around the world who continue to think money might buy them freedom.

ANTI-SOCIAL MEDIA

One of the striking features of modern life is our ability to get a glimpse into the lives of others. Social media forums like Facebook, Twitter and personal blogs do bring many of us closer. What many people don't understand, however, is that these forums only give us part of a story. In essence, they let us see what the poster wants us to see.

On Facebook, for example, people commonly share photos of themselves jet setting around the world, attending fabulous parties, hobnobbing with the elite and generally living a great life.

The deeper truth of their lives is not found in what people say, it's in what they don't say. It's those silent spaces I'm interested in.

There's always something unspoken about every story, even (and often especially) those stories that show only how amazing and perfect someone's life is. While there are some notable exceptions of real and vulnerable online people, generally what you get on social media is more persona than person.

The ugly truth of social media is that it magnifies the opportunities to compare ourselves against others, typically in a negative light. But comparing ourselves to others is not a phenomenon that started with social media. People have been comparing themselves to others for a long time. Social media just magnifies that practice, which is precisely why I think it should be called anti-social media.

If honesty is what makes us vulnerable (an important component to authenticity), then social media typically supports the opposite. At a recent keynote speech in Silicon Valley California, I told the audience, "I hope you are half as happy as you pretend you are on Facebook every day." The audience laughed, but I wondered how many heard the message.

Time magazine ran a poll recently which asked the following questions:

1. Do you believe that on social-media profiles, other people make themselves look happier, more attractive and more successful than they really are? A staggering 76% of people said 'yes'.
2. Do you believe your social-media profile reflects what you're really like? An even more staggering 78% 'yes'.

SOMEONE ELSE'S LIFE

While it's funny to joke about online fakers and the epidemic of comparing ourselves to others, and then pretend we'd never do that, the risk of basing opinions on false assumptions is a lot less funny in real life. At a workshop I conducted in Vancouver, I tried to get participants to think about just how much we believe someone else's life is superior to our own. What I observed was astonishing. Let me explain . . . The workshop I'm talking about has become known as the "Someone Else's Life" Base Camp. As the weekend progressed, it was obvious that each person in the room would prefer their life to be like someone else's in the room.

Seeing people desire what someone else has (or appears to have) isn't new to me. What was unique this time around was that the thing each person wanted was something that someone else in the room already had. The people in the room believed they needed this thing so badly that many described it as the thing necessary to their own happiness.

Take Bob, for example. He was a workshop participant who wanted nothing more than to build his dream house out in the country on 10 gorgeous acres that overlooked a river and was surrounded by forest. Bob had imagined this home down to the finest detail. He'd also gone to the point of having blueprints drawn up for the house of his dreams.

That particular day, Bob expressed sadness because he hadn't yet reached his goal. Indeed, he was quite a distance from reaching it. Some of his investments hadn't been profitable, and he'd failed to get the pay raise he expected. Now his dream of the perfect house was at risk—along with his happiness.

Across the room sat Mike. He was agape as he listened to Bob describe this dream home. At that time, Mike was already living in a home eerily similar to what Bob described. Mike had worked on the goal for many years, struggled to get the money together, dreamed about it, planned it, and finally achieved it.

If the workshop was about achieving goals, then Mike's wisdom to Bob might have been to keep at it, struggle harder and continue down the same path. But as the workshop was about getting down to the truth, Mike's actual message to Bob was that the big house wasn't worth it. Mike told Bob the home hadn't delivered happiness. In fact, it had been a huge burden on his life and was even causing financial stress.

Another man was a full-time investor and another was a wanna-be pro soccer player. Across the room sat a man whose life goal was to quit his job and become a full-time investor—and a woman who'd played soccer for Team Canada at the World Cup. The full-time investor and accomplished soccer players both said their lives weren't any better as a result.

Participants in this particular group were like a microcosm of the larger society. Their experiences illustrated that many people hold goals, dreams and aspirations in common with other people. In and of themselves, these goals are neither right nor wrong. There is no moral standard. Attachment to specific goals, however, can be unhealthy.

Each person at that workshop had a deeply-held belief that once their goal was realized, they'd be happy. Think about that for a moment: people believe they couldn't be happy until a goal was realized. That concept foreshadows the harm in this way of thinking. If everything good lies in the future, what are we to do with the present?

This future orientation is an epidemic. It took hold all across Ireland during the Celtic Tiger and it happens every day, in every town and city, in every continent. This epidemic is the underlying topic of this book. This book is not about giving up on dreams and aspirations. It is all about taking responsibility to identify the real meaning behind the things we say we want.

I've had the remarkable honour of working with incredible people. Their stories have inspired me to the core. Why? Because I've seen how people can make the shift from being poor on life to being rich on life.

The people in this book are just like you and I. They're real people who want something more from their life. Most of them sought a better life outside of themselves before learning how to find a better life from within.

This book is about coming back to yourself. Whatever your personal situation and wherever you are at this moment, you can come back to yourself and find the gem of you. As with the remarkable people in this book, you can deepen your connection with yourself and become more authentic to yourself each and every day. It's the most difficult and rewarding journey of your lifetime. If this book can spur you to enter your journey from where you stand at this moment, I will be more than thrilled.

This book may challenge the authenticity of the dreams and goals that got you to this point in your life. I don't want you to spend years chasing an inauthentic goal that you think will make you happy, only to disappoint you when you achieve it.

I stood by and watched millions of my countrymen and countrywomen become rich on paper while ignoring the things that could make them truly happy. They didn't set out to be unhappy. But they did allow themselves to be intoxicated by the fumes of what they erroneously believed would bring them "success." Like it or not, most of them willingly paid an unhealthy Social Invoice because they put money ahead of meaning.

The people you are about to read about are all individuals I have met and, in many cases, worked with. While their names and some details have been changed to protect their privacy, their stories are real. In using their stories, I'm not suggesting they've "arrived." It's not possible to be "done" working on ourselves. We can only seek to improve from one day to the next. What really matters is that they had the courage to change, the courage to grow.

I commend every one of these people for working on themselves, and for seeking to make real change, to become more aware of who they are, and to lean into their life's journey with all their hearts. In a world that values inauthenticity, they were inspired to live an authentic life.

WHO IS PADRAIG HARRINGTON, AND WHAT DOES HE HAVE TO DO WITH ME?

Padraig Harrington is one of the greatest Irish golfers in history. I have a personal connection to him, as Padraig played for a number of Irish teams my own father captained and selected.

One of Padraig's most notable accomplishments in golf is that, along with Tiger Woods, Padraig is one of the few men to win back-to-back championships at the British Open championship in the past century. Padraig also won three major championships in a period of 18 months, another rarity.

But Padraig did something even more remarkable as a young man, something that most people, even his fans, don't know about. What did he do? He faced the truth. When Padraig was 15 years old, he believed he had a majestic golf swing. One day, a coach videoed his swing and the young golfer was shattered by what he saw in the video. His swing was uncoordinated, jerky, ugly and ineffective.

Then he made a remarkable decision. Rather than continue to believe his own false perception, he set out to completely overhaul his swing. As painful as it was for him to look at the truth and adapt accordingly, he knew it was the only way to get better. I often say perception is nothing, truth is everything. Padraig chose the truth with stunning results.

I share this example of Padraig to illustrate how many people get stuck on this first level of self-growth by refusing to see the truth of their current situation. They can only see their own life through the several filters they themselves have made. Those who keep an open mind and open heart when reading these stories will position themselves to enable the stories and the lessons to sink in. This is essential to digging a bit deeper into your own story and into your own journey. When we look beyond the filters, we allow ourselves to see what's really possible.

FINDING YOUR VOICE

Finding your own voice, never mind your own path, is hard work in a world shouting at you from all directions to perform and conform. The world wants you and me to step into line with the rest of society.

We're brought up to believe that those with a formal education will get jobs that pay better. We're encouraged to climb the ladder of success with the assumption that it's the way to the Promised Land of fulfillment, abundance, and happiness. (No wonder we get so confused when economic anomalies like the Celtic Tiger come into our lives!)

In our society, the line between *who we are* and *what we do* has been blurred, if not erased. Many people, if not most, define themselves by what they do professionally. What they *do* becomes who they *are*.

Assuming what you do is deeply aligned to who you are at the core, this would not be all bad. But most of us are not so "aligned." And this apparent disconnect can be confusing. Do you ever catch yourself thinking of yourself as your title, or your position, rather than as a whole person? This is the central problem and the idea that informed this book, *Rich on Paper, Poor on Life*.

The crux of the issue is simple. While we identify (or believe we are supposed to identify) with our position, rank, and title, research shows many of us don't even like the jobs that we have allowed to define us. A major survey conducted recently by the *Deloitte Shift Index* notes that 80% of people hate their jobs—but are too scared to do anything about it. The report suggests that this fear is driven by a challenging global economic climate. This rationale is rubbish.

After travelling to almost 70 countries and working with thousands of people, I believe that in the developed world the 80/20 rule can be applied to the three elements of people's lives: Work, Self, and Others. These three areas will be discussed in depth later, so don't worry if you don't know exactly what I mean when I mention them now. At this point, what you need to understand is that 80% of people are *settling* in at least one of the three areas. By settling, I mean they are "making do" with the status quo. While that might seem practical, it's also problematic because the vast majority does not even know they are settling.

These individuals are not fulfilled by the lives they lead. Still, they move through the world entirely unaware of what they might do to improve their relationships with Work, Self and Others. Worse, many don't believe they deserve any better. I want to challenge those notions. If it's true that we settle most in work and in relationships, I believe it's time to ask why that's the case.

It is often said that one of the biggest causes of relationship breakups is money. Again, I don't buy this explanation. I acknowledge the idea that financial pressure might present the straw that breaks the proverbial camel's back. But that straw is not, in and of itself, the biggest problem. Just think about it. Financial pressure is debilitating. But the underlying cracks that appear when financial pressure is added to a relationship, were there before the money problems were piled on top of the weakened foundation.

The added weight contributes to the problem—but should not be confused with the root cause of the shaky foundation. The ugly truth of relationships in trouble is that most people involved never deal with the core issues. Many don't even recognize the real problems. Instead, they just blame their breakup on the only thing they can put their finger on—money.

Sometimes the "family economy" is the only thing that holds a troubled relationship together. That doesn't make the relationship better. It does prove that people will settle for money.

We also settle in work. We're brought up in a society that claims to want what's "best" for us. Unfortunately, that perspective disguises the problem by limiting our options to what's "best" within a narrowly-defined list of choices. Again, we perform—and conform. And why not? Since we crave acceptance so deeply, it makes sense that we busy ourselves with the daily activity of pleasing others. In work, we settle for acceptance.

The end result of this willingness to accept and even pursue the status quo is what leads us to adopt personal and professional goals based on mental constructs that don't belong to us in the first place. Instead, these ideas belong to our parents, our friends, or society. We are fooled into thinking they represent what we want. Deep down, in the core of our beings, they represent the polar opposite.

This encourages us to pursue what we think we want. And that's a tragedy, since what we think we want is almost always different from what we really *need*. To understand why our wants and needs are so often in conflict, we need to ask why it's so difficult to stand up for who you are and what you believe.

The real issue is fear. We are afraid of judgment. Indeed, we crave acceptance to an unhealthy point. We know there's a spark deep inside—something the world hasn't yet seen, but the fear of not fitting in is so strong we'd rather put up with the status quo than run the risk of being happy.

If you don't believe me, ask yourself where you've been settling. Are you doing the work you'd dreamed of as a child? Do your primary relationships resemble the relationships you want? Are you as healthy as you imagined? Are you as vital? Do you find satisfaction and joy in your friendships and family relationships?

We settle in all these areas—and more.

WHEN WORK'S NOT ENOUGH

A client of mine once sat before me sharing about how much he hated his job. He'd been thinking about it for years, and his mission was to quit. He wanted to remove himself from the drudgery of his day-to-day existence. This was the way he described it, not me.

I asked if he could think of something he'd like more. Slowly he said, "Um, I don't know, maybe fishing?"

We talked about what fishing was to him, and he explained that he not only loved fishing for himself, he loved taking others on fishing expeditions. Living in the Vancouver area, this man particularly enjoyed taking people sturgeon fishing. He loved seeing their joy at landing a monster sturgeon.

Now, I'm not into fishing, but I'm told this species dates back to the time of the dinosaurs, and that catching a sturgeon is a stunning experience. In the Fraser River, which runs through Vancouver and into the Pacific Ocean, White Sturgeon grow bigger than anywhere else on earth, with some reaching 12 feet in length. Listening to this client talk about fishing gave me special insight into how I could help him find his voice.

The problem for this man was that he felt enormous pressure to make something of his life. Fishing, even though it was about giving pleasure to other people, simply wasn't enough. While this man's self-belief process is still evolving, I know that he feels a sense of empowerment from speaking his truth. I hope he continues to step further into his speaking his truth, and that he learns not to discount the pleasure he gets from sharing fishing experiences with others.

And that's what I want for you, too. This book was written to inspire you to rediscover—and reignite—that spark within. It is meant to help you discover what you really want to do—and to celebrate all that makes you special. In a world that wants you to be ordinary, the ideas in this book launch a journey towards the exceptional.

But there is work to be done. To make authentic and sustainable change in your life, the change must come from within. To illustrate how this process works best, I have chosen stories that demonstrate how this kind of change is the organic outcome of a natural process that begins when individuals commit to leading a more authentic life.

All of which makes this a Must Do book versus a How To book. So listen up. This is a call to listen to your inner voice. At this point in your journey, that voice might be little more than a whisper. But fear not. Even the faintest voice deserves reverence—and listening carefully is where your Must Do begins.

And fear not: this tour is guided, and I know it works because I've seen it transform lives over and over again.

LET'S GET STARTED

This book tells 15 real-life stories[1] to rattle the mind and stir the soul in the quest to bring more meaning into your life. Throughout, I'll share the "big picture" truths I've gleaned from the work I've done with Olympic athletes, TV personalities, professional soccer players, couples, corporations and, most

---

[1] Each story is based on a real person and their real story but the names and details have been changed to protect each person's anonymity.

importantly, the individuals who had the courage to believe there was more. These stories include the tale of an investor who discovered that authenticity was the best business strategy he could ever use. You'll also be introduced to a guy whose quest for authenticity enabled him to realize his lifelong dream of becoming a professional music producer, performer and teacher, simply by doing the self-work this book is designed to teach you.

What these stories all have in common is the process these people followed. Every one of them peeled back the layers and took off the masks that were affecting the three elements of Work, Self, and Others. The end result was clarity about the lives they led and the lives they wanted to live, as well as the courage to make real change towards living those lives.

While there is no substitute for self-work, this book will ensure you're moving towards your authentic path. It will show you ways to turn down the screaming voices that tell you to conform and fit in. It will help you hear the whisper in your soul.

All of us have a lot of reasons to stick to the path we've already taken. I urge you to start this new journey today. You don't want to be the person who lives a life of regret and disappointment. You want to be the person who listens to the whisper of your soul—and takes action on the transformative wisdom of its message. In sum, you want to be like the people you'll meet in this book. So read on—and read on with an open mind and an open heart. This book will help you identify your blind spots, gain clarity on the path ahead and unlock the courage I know you already have inside. This is your time—take it.

> *"Be yourself; everyone else is already taken."*
> *~ Oscar Wilde*

PART ONE:
WORK

YOUR RELATIONSHIP TO WHAT YOU DO

"Perception is nothing, the truth is everything."
~ *Philip McKernan*

DOING VERSUS BEING HAPPY

I don't believe any human deserves to be happy, but most people think it's a god-given right. This sense of entitlement dilutes the authentic drive for happiness. I find it fascinating that people who spend eight hours a day doing work they do not believe in, wonder why they don't feel complete. Often I see people putting their mortgage ahead of meaning, and justifying it to themselves like only humans can do best.

Many of the bills people "have to pay" result from the decisions they made when putting money ahead of their well-being in the first place. It is a dangerous cycle. Never before in the history of humanity have we had the opportunity to do what we love and make money doing it. I believe our work must be an extension of what we believe, not of who we think we are. We now *consume* happiness rather than live happily. And no, I'm not talking about frequent trips to McDonald's.

The line between being and doing happy is blurred. Consuming happiness tricks us into thinking we are happy when really we're acting. Doing happy has us consuming experiences like a trip to the movies or a vacation to Disney. This provides a temporary escape to a happier place, but does not deal with the reality that most aren't fulfilled.

Being happy on the other hand is being in a great relationship, having a healthy relationship with oneself, with others and doing the work we love. This first section is focused on work, but as you'll see throughout the book, all three parts of life are connected as they relate to our happiness.

CHAPTER 1:

TAKING BUSINESS TO THE NEXT LEVEL

"Many people spend more time, money, and energy trying to grow their net worth than they do on their self-worth."
~ Philip McKernan

UNAUTHENTIC EXTERNAL GOALS

Have you ever written down a set of goals? If so, did you expect to achieve every goal on the list and reach instant happiness? Have you been taught somewhere along the way about the alchemical magic of goal-setting?

Well, join the club. Goal-setting has been an obsession with our success-oriented culture for a long time and many of us have been sucked into its vortex.

I'm not against advancing in the direction of your choosing. Nor do I think it's necessarily a bad practice to write out targets. But there's a big caveat to goal-setting. The ugly truth is that many people chase goals that are not theirs. And what's the point of chasing someone elses or society's goals?

As you learned with the example of the Celtic Tiger in Ireland, the problem of people being rich on paper and poor on life is an epidemic. One of the reasons for this is the false appropriation of goals. Let me introduce you to Emma. As you read through her story, think about why she pursued goals that weren't her own and a dream that didn't belong to her.

THE ARCHITECT

During the early years of the Celtic Tiger phenomenon, I met with an architect named Emma. At the time, Emma maintained a small but in-demand architectural firm, designing homes and add-ons for her clients. Based in Dublin, she was taking on projects as she wanted, yet able to turn down projects she didn't have the time or interest to pursue. She was busy, but in control of her time.

Emma invited me to her home, where her office was based, for coffee and a discussion. As we chatted, it became clear that she wanted to focus only on the future.

When I insisted upon speaking about her current reality, she began to paint me a picture of her current life and business. I asked her what she liked about her current business and she told me how her favourite part was listening and interacting with her clients, taking their ideas and designing them into a beautiful reality. The process of taking a project from concept to fruition brought her enormous joy.

In fact, she lit up as she described a recently completed extension to a home. It was clear: creating something that (in turn) created joy in others' lives was at the core of her passion.

Emma spent many hours with her clients brainstorming ideas, developing concepts, testing them, and refining the vision. Since Emma was highly sought after in her niche market, she hand-picked her clients with great care.

Many of Emma's clients were wealthy. They were also often busy within their various roles in business or as directors of companies. For Emma and her clients, the opportunity to create beautiful spaces was a tremendously fulfilling outlet for creative energy. With a growing reputation for quality work and collaboration, Emma's business was poised to grow.

As part of the discovery process, I also asked Emma to describe a typical day in her life. Emma explained how she'd wake up every morning, practice yoga, and then enjoy a relaxing breakfast before making herself a cup of coffee. Once the coffee was ready, she'd walk down the corridor to a small studio she'd designed and built in her backyard. Her eyes twinkled when she told me her coffee was still hot when she arrived at her desk. Since I was sitting in her lovely home at the time, I had no trouble imagining the entire scene, hot coffee and all.

Upon "commuting" to her garden office, Emma spent her day creating, collaborating, and designing. At lunchtime, she walked back down the corridor to the kitchen, ate a healthy meal, relaxed for a little while, and then returned to her studio.

Next, we discussed money, and Emma told me that she was making good money. In terms of material wealth, she lived in the home she designed to meet all of her needs. She'd also saved up a nice little nest egg and had made a few solid investments.

Financially, this architect was well off. She was turning over more than $300,000 per year and retaining a healthy portion of that.

Emma made a comfortable living, regularly indulged her hobbies, travelled, and still had a significant amount of money left over to invest.

Her current reality at the time was quite wonderful, but she'd asked to meet because she wanted something to change. When speaking on the phone before that first meeting, Emma told me she wanted to go the "next level."

After she described her current reality, I turned the conversation around and asked her what she meant by that the "next level." I soon learned she wanted to double her turnover. Her new benchmark for sales was $600,000, which she wanted to achieve the following year.

After making her desire for double turnover clear, Emma and I continued our conversation. I focused the conversation on what was needed to double her turnover. In sum, Emma would need to take on more customers and larger projects. This would necessitate that she hire at least one additional architect, maybe two.

Hiring another architect would also change Emma's other staff requirements. She would need at least one support staff member to handle payroll, bookkeeping, accounts receivable, accounts payable, and systems.

I asked her what each day would be like for *her* in terms of client work. She thought she'd still get to do quite a lot of the client work she loves. She did recognize that she would have to spend more time networking, marketing, and selling in order to bring in the new clients and pay additional staff.

As she talked, it became apparent to me that the new architects on staff would have to conduct many of the face-to-face meetings Emma now enjoyed with her clients. She also told me the new architect would handle many of the new drawings that had to be made. Ergo, Emma's drawing time would be minimized. While Emma still didn't "hear" what she was really saying, I started to see the potential issues.

Then we spoke about her work environment. I asked if she'd operate the entire business, which we agreed would include at least three staff members, from the same home office. After a moment's thought, Emma surmised that she'd have to get an office in an industrial park about 30 minutes away.

Knowing that a life well-lived (and well-enjoyed) is in the details, I asked her if her coffee would still be hot by the time she got to that new office. As traffic jams were a common part of Celtic Tiger life, Emma admitted that even in an insulated cup her coffee would be, at best, warm. Convinced that coffee was a minor detail, Emma still wanted to get to the next level.

And so, we continued . . .

NEXT LEVEL SYNDROME (NLS)

But something had changed. Talking about coffee helped Emma realize the changes she was talking about were not minor details. She had worked hard to get herself in the position of living the dream life. She thought she wanted more, but she hadn't really considered what it would cost her to double her receipts. With new information on the table, Emma's plan was put in question. Emma said she didn't want to give up the face-to-face time with her clients or the days spent immersed in drawing and creation. She also started to question whether she wanted to give up her

30-second stroll down the corridor to her garden studio. These were, after all, the very activities she loved most about her work.

This guided conversation helped Emma understand she already had something greater than what next level offered. Her quest for more money now threatened her happiness, fulfillment, meaning, and peace of mind.

Once Emma re-evaluated her ambition, she started to look at *why* she'd developed those goals. That's when Emma realized money was the only *why*. Upon further reflection, she acknowledged she didn't even have plans for what the extra money might buy. Emma was already doing the things she wanted to do!

Emma's example is not unusual. Her social circle was full of people in pursuit of the next level, and this same more-money-is-better mentality was sweeping the globe, too. It even spawned an entire industry of gurus who convinced their followers of the need to pursue the next level. How sad. The authentic truth is that what the next level looks like can be very seductive. A fast car, beautiful spouse, and a home on a beautiful island can look pretty good to those who know they want to make changes in their lives. And don't get me wrong. I am not against growth in your business, or money. My argument is against growth for growth's sake, and money for money's sake. All I'm saying is that if you think your business needs to grow, consider the real facts of what that growth will foster.

First, do not trade in a lifestyle you love for a lifestyle that you would love a lot less. Emma already had a dream lifestyle. She travelled. She lived in a lovely home. She didn't commute. She had time to practice yoga and eat healthy meals. She had time to relax, every day. Growing her business would have resulted in some big changes to her lifestyle.

Another caveat is that you understand *why* you want to grow your business before trying to embark on a path of growth. Was there anything about turning over $600,000 that would've made Emma's life any better than it was with $300,000? If there was, she couldn't name it when we spoke. She just wanted more for the sake of more.

Some people are convinced they need more money to do the things they want. For example, many people want to give back by helping, volunteering, and taking care of others. It's a beautiful dream I fully support. Giving back is fulfilling, and in many ways is the pinnacle of a life well-lived. But you don't need $600,000 in sales to give back. In reality, the people who nurture a massive vision for transforming the world often miss the boat by never going out and just helping *one* individual. It's so simple to give back, but we complicate the hell out of it.

> *"As humans we're masters of two things;*
> *complicating our lives and justifying why we did it."*
> *~ Philip McKernan*

A third caveat is that you should not budge an inch off of what you love about the work you do in order to get to the next level. If you're an architect like Emma, and you love the client interactions and the drawings, then why would you give those up for more money?

It's what we do on a daily basis that provides us with peace of mind and meaning. NLS causes more suffering in the working world than we imagine. There are millions of talented individuals who've given up what they love about their jobs or businesses for more money. Without exception, they all end up unhappy and unfulfilled. Worse yet, many of them receive their Social Invoice in the daily mail.

And here's the saddest part about these misguided efforts at growth: businesses grow organically when the owner does more of what they love. When you grow your business by out-sourcing the parts you love, you risk finding yourself tied to work you dislike, perhaps even detest. No wonder so many people find it tough to get out of bed!

In summary, Emma was one of the lucky ones. By rethinking her approach, she grounded her business (and herself) in a strategy that was already working well.

THE WRONG REASONS

What I really want you to think about is the immense power in asking the simple question, "Why?"

When I asked Emma why she wanted to go to the next level, she had many very *logical* reasons why pushing for the next level would make sense. And I have no doubt that from a standard notion of success and fulfillment, seeking the next level makes a great deal of sense to most.

However, it's not until we begin to *feel* the next level that we begin to realize it's not all it's cracked up to be. Once Emma imagined the changes her ambitious business plan would bring about, she realized the next level might not be as great as she'd first imagined.

Many people achieve what they set out when they make, set, and achieve big goals. But what they end up with is often different from what they imagined. Indeed, it's rare to find a person who's achieved all of the so-called success, and not damaged him or herself and their relationships along the way. I've seen it with my own eyes. Getting caught up the NLS is a short cut to being rich on paper, but poor on life.

Emma dodged that bullet by being real with herself.

CHAPTER 2:

GIVING UP YOUR BABY

*"The past has created the present
and the present is creating the future."*
~ *Philip McKernan*

PEDESTALS AND SELF-WORTH

Have you ever felt that a friend, family member, or even someone you've never met was somehow above you, better than you or more capable than you? The vast majority of people would answer yes to this question.

This tendency to put other people on pedestals is directly linked to the Next Level Syndrome and problems caused by setting inauthentic goals.

Let me explain how. One of the ways we develop inauthentic goals and NLS is by a lack of self-belief. Since we don't believe in ourselves, we start attaching ourselves to goals. We do this because we think that achieving certain goals will make us better or more worthy. That lack of self-belief often leads us to put others on a pedestal. This confirms that we are "lesser than."

It also fuels the development of inauthentic goal setting. To paraphrase Sir Walter Scott, "Oh what tangled webs we weave when first we practice to deceive—ourselves."

PUTTING THE PRESIDENT ON A PEDESTAL

Remember my story about caddying for the President of Ireland? Once I found my voice that day, I was able to help him make better shots. But why did I wait?

Even as a child, I'd already internalized messages about putting people like the President on a pedestal. This predilection for putting others on top of pedestals is something I really (really) want people to think about. How can anyone find their voice while putting others on a pedestal?

That tendency to put others on a pedestal compromises our ability to be real. And that reduces our ability to be vulnerable, even though it's essential to being authentic.

I don't know if that fear of vulnerability has an evolutionary explanation in the basic fight/flight response of human beings, but I do know the fear is real. In the personal growth arena, it's the people who break through that barrier, the people who make the biggest changes in their lives allow themselves to be vulnerable. And how can that not happen? People who stop "acting" their way through life become more authentic. That helps them remove people from pedestals, and the more you remove people from pedestals, the less you feel the need to act.

Am I 100% authentic? Have I found 100% of my voice? The answer to both is no. However, I can say that I'm more authentic now than ever before, and that working to be even more authentic matters to me. It's no coincidence that most of the people I used to put on pedestals no longer occupy those treasured places. I am enough.

TARA'S TALE

Tara is an entrepreneurial client who shares many characteristics with Emma. She had created an in-demand and passion-based business that enabled her to fashion an amazing lifestyle. The business supported the lifestyle, and the lifestyle made it easy for her to optimize her business. Tara was happy. By the time she took some time off to have her first child, the successful web software engineer had chalked up five years as the top performing employee in a successful San Francisco-based company.

After her second child was born, Tara decided she wanted to go back to working a less hectic schedule. She also knew she didn't want to go back to working five or six days per week. What she needed was a work/life balance that would allow her to develop her business and spend time with her children.

Tara's first goal was to work three days per week. Realizing it might be difficult to find a position with the flexibility she needed, she decided to launch her own company. Unlike Emma, who didn't like the idea of leading a team, Tara loved that part of her business. Having already built a reputation for leading others, Tara envisioned a company where she could employ or contract other software engineers. According to her vision, many of these designers would also be parents working from home offices. Her vision was to first create the work and lifestyle balance for herself, then replicate the system and welcome contract employees. That powerful sense of *why* is what drove Tara's business plan.

By the time I met Tara, her business had been operational for FIVE years. She was doing her own projects and had other engineers working for her on contract. There were challenges, but the business was doing well.

TARA'S NEXT LEVEL

Tara's accomplishments were impressive. She went into the business with a passion for creation and project leadership. But she wasn't an expert at marketing, internal systems, or business management.

When Tara reached out to me, she admitted to feeling like her business had plateaued. She even confessed to being a bit bored. Loving a good challenge, she decided to grow her business to $5M in sales per year—all while maintaining her three-day week. As targets go, Tara's plan made logical sense given what she knew about demand for her companys' services.

As the jump was significant, Tara rightfully believed she'd need some help to get there. It didn't take her long to find a highly experienced and successful prospective partner to help with marketing and systems. As she had a personal history with the individual, Tara was flattered by his keen interest. Although she wanted to retain majority ownership, she was willing to let the partner buy-in and own up to 49% of the company.

When he wanted more, Tara gave in. What she didn't do is ask why she was willing to accept a deal that went against her own business plan. And that's too bad because, as you'll soon find out, an honest answer to that question would have prevented a lot of problems.

AN INCH OR A MILE

Let me digress. A few years back, I had an experience similar to Tara's. While nobody was offering to buy into my business, I did have the opportunity to integrate myself with a much larger organization. The experience taught me a valuable lesson: when you believe another person or business can make you better by partnering or joining in with them, you risk undervaluing yourself.

The issue is simple. Whenever you put someone else on a pedestal, regardless of how much height you give that podium, the end structure is lop-sided. It's bizarre when you think about it. Why would you not be as good as someone else? It's bizarre, but so widespread. I don't know many people who don't struggle with this on some level, and we often don't think there's anything wrong with this. Believing others are better than us isn't merely a common way of thinking, it's often confused with basic good manners.

Think about it. Do you ever regard other people and assume you could never do what they do? Do you ever think others must be better than you—often on the fundamentally flawed rationale of what they have or consume? Most people can name, with remarkably little reflection, people they would put on a pedestal.

This was true in my own life. I came within a hair's width of joining my business with a much larger organization simply because I had put the leaders of that organization on a pedestal. While I didn't understand it at first, that act assumed I needed those people to succeed or further my career.

Tara faced a similar problem. In spite of her skill and hard-earned success, Tara suffered from self-doubt. It was this lack of self-

belief that led her to put the new business pa
even though the deal he offered compromise
I'm not suggesting a partnership wasn't the
take. Determined to expand her business,
her own weaknesses in trying to go it alone. The busin〜〜
would bring what the business needed to grow.

But the strong *why* wasn't enough. Because Tara was contemplating a partnership with someone she'd put on a pedestal, she was devaluing herself. As is often the case, Tara was so enamoured with the new partner she didn't even realize what was happening! That changed at a mentoring weekend Tara attended. I was leading the group through a simple exercise where I asked the group to consider who in their life they had on a pedestal. After ten minutes of thought, participants discussed who they had on a pedestal. When it was Tara's turn to talk, she admitted that putting her business partner on a pedestal was the primary reason she'd been willing to accept a deal that wasn't as good as she wanted.

REAL PASSION FOR BUSINESS

> "When it comes to the work you do please don't confuse excitement for passion. It could cost you your health, relationships, and your peace of mind."
> ~ Philip McKernan

Passion, as it relates to business, is a misunderstood concept. In our great desire to live a passionate life, we often take something we don't actually have a passion for and convince ourselves we do. I see this all the time. Over the years, I've worked with hundreds of entrepreneurs. This tendency to confuse excitement with passion is common within the entrepreneurial community.

ever I question these passionate entrepreneurs a bit
per, I often find they often don't really have a passion for their
business at all!

What's going on? Simply put, many of them believe their business
will give them freedom. Upon further questioning, I discover the
kind of freedom is not defined. They may talk about "financial
freedom," but they're not even sure what that means. With few
exceptions, these entrepreneurs' deepest desire is something
other than the business they're currently operating. They usually
want time with loved ones, freedom to travel the world, time to
help others or time to pursue their art. They believe their business
will help them get to a place where they can finally do this thing
they love.

Logically, this makes sense. It's another version of the story
we've been sold our whole lives. If we work hard now, we'll be
able to retire later. When we retire we'll be able to do all the
things we can't do now. Logical or not, it's also self-defeating for
entrepreneurs to try and convince themselves something is their
passion if it isn't. More often than not they're feeling excitement,
not passion.

By holding the false belief that a certain business is their passion,
these individuals aren't able to pursue the activities that will
actually create a life that allows them to live their true passion.

Because some have misconstrued my message, I want to be clear.
I'm not suggesting entrepreneurs should drop everything and
give up their business. But they do need to understand that their
business has a place, and they need to be prepared to put it there.

If you're an entrepreneur who wants to spend more time with
family, practice art or travel, *then by all means do those things*. But

do it now! Don't wait for an imagined future where business has taken away all your concerns, and please don't pretend a certain business is your passion if it isn't. This might seem simple and obvious, but I've met many people who've mistakenly confused excitement with passion.

Here's how we end up on the wrong path. Most people take a job because they have to. Before long, they discover they don't really love their job. In fact, many of them actually hate what they do. With studies showing that 80% of people hate their jobs, I'm hardly over-stating the fact when I say that hating one's job is more the rule than the exception.

Nevertheless, people work because they have to work, and before long they settle into the job because it provides a living. They accept the false belief that all work is drudgery and the idea that they will be doing this job until they retire. Confronted with the awareness that they may never get to do what they really want to do, some of these individuals will start to believe entrepreneurial activities, like real estate, for example, represents their only hope out of the drudgery. What many of them don't realize is that this new-found "passion" for an entrepreneurial endeavor is really founded on the "excitement" of switching up the drudgery. (They don't really want to do the work of an entrepreneur—but it sure sounds exciting!) This desire to lead a more interesting work life isn't limited to those who claim an entrepreneurial vision. Many of us know dentists, accountants, doctors and lawyers who answered society's call to pursue socially-prestigious professions—and regret it.

What you need to understand is that when it comes to work, many pretend, but few actually live their passion. That's why it's so refreshing to see someone who is *truly* passionate about his or her work. I find it often shows up with entrepreneurs who enjoy the core *activity* of their business. These include entrepreneurs like Emma and Tara from Chapters one and two, respectively.

"Excitement is a freeing break from the norm that's described with words to try and capture its essence. Passion is a part of your soul, which ignites a fire in your belly, resulting in a spark in your eyes."
~ *Philip McKernan*

I framed the passion discussion in the context of Tara's story because I believe she does have a passion-based business. She loves the creative process, not just the result. And her love of the process includes project leadership. Tara genuinely enjoys helping others work together to create something new. With all that fire in her eyes and spark in her belly, why was Tara willing to give up so much of her business?

Why Did She Have The Partner On a Pedestal?

And this is where Tara's story offers the biggest lessons. The bottom line is that Tara's partner's resume had almost nothing to do with her decision to put him on a pedestal. On the contrary, Tara's actions are 100% about how Tara felt about herself.

Why would Tara have a lack of self-belief? She had already achieved a great deal of success with the company she developed and in her former work as an employee. Academically speaking, she'd also succeeded in university and, before, at high school. Her personal life was also solid. Tara felt good about who she was as a wife and mother, and she took credit for how she managed those roles alongside her business. So what was the problem?

DIGGING INTO OUR STORY

The best way to answer that question is to get in touch with our own stories, and I can give you an example from my own life. I spent my entire youth living in fear of school. While there, I would sit in class with a knot in my stomach hoping that the teacher wouldn't call on me. When it did happen, I often found a way to get out of the situation. I became a master of bluffing my way through.

I did this because I couldn't read. Moreover, the fear and shame of being exposed as illiterate drove me to do everything I could to avoid reading aloud in class.

Whenever I revisit my own story, I recall the countless hours I spent trying to keep myself from going insane in classes where I simply wasn't able to learn. I actually remember counting the pieces of dandruff on the back of the student in front of me for what felt like days. And let me say, this was also ingenious as a strategy. That kid's back was the perfect height for my eyes. If I looked up, I risked catching the teacher's eye. If looked down at the floor, I'd draw attention to myself as not paying attention.

Being unable to read fluently affected everything I did. With the help of one very special teacher and a lot of work, I've since learned how to read much better. That said, I still have a great deal of anxiety about reading and writing. The crux of the problem is that most of the teachers I encountered heaped ridicule on me. In fairness, few of them had any understanding of the real problem. Rather than admit my disability, I put on masks to disguise the problem—and my fear. Because I believed I was unteachable, I allowed them to think the same.

Coming to terms with this aspect of my own story has given me great insight into why I am so passionate about the work I do. Because I now realized how my own masks held me back, I'm hyper-aware of the masks other people wear. I also know that some of these masks are donned without conscious thought. Sometimes we wear them just to get through the day!

As I got older, I learned that I had an aptitude for talking to people and for sales. As these were activities *prized* by society, my confidence grew. I wasn't a natural-born scholar, but I found success in my early business ventures and that success had an unexpected (and intriguing) effect. My reading and writing may have still been problematic—but people were genuinely interested in hearing me talk about my business success and what it took to overcome dyslexia.

Which doesn't mean my life has been a bed of roses. Along the way, I entered into some ill-fated partnerships. My dyslexia, combined with my decades-long habit of wearing masks, drove me into some ill-fated partnerships. Like Tara, I put business partners on pedestals because my own self-doubt led me to see them as more important. Understanding my story allowed me to stop that practice. I now see that the tendency to put others on pedestals came from my deep need for acceptance. I'd been wearing masks for so long that I didn't even know who I was, let alone what I might be capable of accomplishing.

REMOVING THE PEDESTAL

Now aware of what she risked by putting the partner on a pedestal, Tara re-assessed the proposed buy-in—and asked for more. Unsurprisingly, the partner agreed and countered with a better offer. The last time I spoke to Tara, she told me, "The new deal saved me millions of dollars."

While that's hard to contest, what really happened is far more important. By demanding a deal that reflected her own true value, Tara pulled her partner from the pedestal. For Tara, as with others in my seminars and workshops, it all comes down to self-belief. If we hold negative false beliefs about our self-worth, we can't help but self-sabotage our efforts to develop our true potential.

CHAPTER 3:

BLIND TO HIS TALENTS

"In the absence of clarity, take action!"
~ Philip McKernan

FALSE BELIEFS, SELF-WORTH, AND TELLING THE WORLD

Have you ever taken an inventory of your beliefs? If so, did you find that all of your beliefs were positive and healthy? Were they even correct? In this chapter, you'll learn about the relationship between false beliefs and self-worth. We'll also look at ways to destroy false beliefs and why taking action, even when you don't have all of the answers, is critical to progress.

FROM PAINTBRUSH TO PEN

Tom arrived at one of my personal mentoring groups a few years ago. While ready for big changes, he had little idea of where he really wanted to go or how those changes might transform his life.

After travelling the world, studying philosophy in university, and working overseas for several years, Tom found himself back in his home city of Calgary, Alberta. With the local and national economy doing well, Tom's dream of business success—and the riches that would follow—seemed entirely in step with what he saw happening all around him. To that end, Tom was learning as much as he could about real estate investments and was about to get his real estate license so he could work as a real estate agent. Professionally speaking, he was moving towards a career in real estate.

When Tom and I met, he hadn't fully transitioned into that line of work. Like so many real estate people that I have met over the years, Tom could talk the talk. He had a "magic number" for how many properties he wanted to own and how much income he expected from his investments. He even had a plan for how he would get to that magic number.

During this transitional period, Tom worked as a house painter to pay the bills. He'd operated a small painting company for two years, doing most of the work himself.

Following my commitment to really get to know my clients, he and I worked through a discovery process that examined Tom's current reality, including his entrepreneurial passion. Tom found it easy to tell me how much he wanted to succeed in the real estate world.

Together, we explored his life and his story. Tom told me that he'd had some difficult experiences within his family. More specifically, he had a half-sibling with whom his family had lost contact. He also had a violent grandfather whose abuse was still an unresolved issue within the family.

In discussing his story, Tom indicated that he'd always wanted to write his grandfather's story. The act would be one of learning, personal growth, and healing. To write the story, Tom would have to learn about his grandfather through the eyes of those who knew him best. At the same time, Tom would also have to face his own feelings of not fitting into the broader family.

From there, we shifted topics to the idea of passion in business. To his credit, Tom eventually admitted that he didn't have a passion for real estate. He admitted that his only interest in real estate was money. That discovery took a while, but to Tom's credit, he soon realized the admission enabled him to question his path. That's important because it also allowed Tom to open his heart and mind up to other possibilities. (When someone is adamant about or attached to what they *think* is the right path, it's almost impossible to get them to even consider other options.)

While it took a number of meetings and some patience on both of our parts to advance an authentic conversation, Tom was eventually ready to answer the question, "If you could do anything at all with no limits, what would it be?" His quick response, "Travel the world and write."

I then asked Tom what doing that work would look like. With some hesitation he continued. Realizing this was a major diversion away from all his earlier claims about building a real estate portfolio and wealth, Tom proposed that helping other people write their own books might be a way to earn money that would enable him to pursue his own writing.

In response to my questions about what that work would involve, Tom told me it would include extensive author interviews followed by writing and revisions. Then he told me that he didn't know if he could do it. Tom wasn't sure if he knew how to do an interview. He didn't know if he could write well enough for publication. He also didn't know if there was enough business to keep him busy as a professional writer.

To follow up his obvious breakthrough, I asked Tom to imagine himself interviewing someone and tell me what some of the questions that he might ask if he were to do it. Without a second thought, Tom rattled off about six great questions.

As Tom's desire to be a writer was deeply buried within, this was a difficult discussion. He struggled to speak openly of his innermost desire. So why did Tom keep talking? Because the discussion revealed a spark he'd never revealed before that day.

And once that had occurred, there was no going back!

TELL THE WORLD

Tom left that meeting without a resolution or grand proclamation to become a writer at all costs. But he carried with him a pulsing sliver of awareness about where his true passions lay. More importantly Tom committed to start writing again.

That process started with a journal. After that, Tom wrote the story of his grandfather, then developed a blog.

Over the years I've been a huge advocate for people to tell the world about their dreams or aspirations. It's like letting a cat out of the bag and once the secret is released, there's no chance of stuffing it back into the bag.

Tom's cat-out-of-the-bag moment prompted someone else in the room to say they needed someone to help them write a book. Sure enough, it was another client winding his way along his own authentic path of discovery. He'd been offered a book contract by a major publisher, but needed a ghost writer's help. Within a few weeks, the two were working together.

Tom admits he struggled with that first book. It was difficult for him to believe that his writing was good enough. He told me later how he'd send part of the manuscript to the editor expecting the editor to respond by firing him for poor work. When the editor (a man with decades of experience in the industry) told him it was great, Tom struggled to believe it. His own self-doubt still held him back.

> *"Thinking big doesn't help, you have to believe big."*
> *~ Philip McKernan*

Tom's lack of inner belief was like the person who "feels" that he or she carries extra weight even when others try to reassure them that's not the case. While Tom had some dark days before he went down the road of becoming a writer, none of those were as dark as those he faced when he started working on his first book. Even though others told him his writing was good—and getting better with practice—Tom's internal demons told him the opposite.

THE NEXT CHAPTER

Even as requests to write more books came his way, Tom found it difficult to believe he was "good enough." He told me about the days he spent sitting in his office without actually doing anything. Tom wasted entire days, then beat himself up for the lack of productivity.

About five months into this process, Tom was having some success on the writing front, but still struggling to put words on paper. He was also working as a real estate agent, a job that allowed him to stop painting, which he hated. Helping clients buy and sell houses meant there were days Tom logged 14 hours as a real estate agent and did not do any writing. Other times, Tom felt good about what he'd written. Those days gave Tom a taste of what it was like to do a job that brought him something he'd never before experienced with his work: joy.

Over time, the time spent on real estate diminished and the time spent writing grew. Tom went from struggling to write 1,000 words in a day to doubling and then tripling that number. As of today, Tom is a full time writer.

PUTTING THE PASSION TO SLEEP

It never ceases to amaze me how millions of people can harbour powerful dreams and never look for ways to bring those dreams to fruition because they simply do not believe in themselves. It saddens me to see people believe in their god without question and yet walk the earth never believing in themselves.

With all of the talk about the importance of passion, we sometimes think "finding your passion" will come from attending a weekend workshop or reading a book. I see this in my own work. Clients come to my shortest weekend workshops and expect to find their passion by the time they leave.

Tom is proof that one can be empowered to take those first real steps towards a dream rather quickly. But it's unrealistic to assume you can "find your passion" in a three-or five-step process. Finding your passion is simply not like looking for a set of keys or a cell phone. My mother was right to tell me that when I lose something, I should retrace my steps until I find it. Finding our passion is entirely different—because we can't find what was never lost.

I think of the process as more of an uncovering or re-discovery. The passion is there all along. It's really a matter of coming back to one's self in order to find it. With Tom, there was immense power in examining his thoughts around his personal history. It allowed him to uncover his dream of writing about his grandfather and that prompted the beginning of his writing journey. Taking up the practice of writing the journal and blog allowed him to experience this passion and discover the joy it brought. Telling the world enabled others to help.

In fairness, Tom's discovery could have gone another way. While he chose to take the knowledge he gained of himself and lean into it, I've seen others gain access to that snippet of self-knowledge, and then run from it.

When passion has been dormant within someone for a long time, it will manifest in numerous ways. With Tom, it showed up with a complete dissatisfaction and disconnect from work. He was painting houses when I first met him. I have nothing against house painters, but you must admit painting houses is a far cry from writing books in this case.

As Tom had a family to care for, he chose to slowly work his way into the writing field. Others do as the Vikings did and burn their ships upon arriving on the uncharted shore. I would be a hypocrite to say that jumping in with both feet is never a good option. I myself have, on a few occasions, been compelled to make a change that may have looked irrational at the time. Perhaps what matters most isn't *how* or *when* you launch your new life, but that you put a plan into place that requires the launching itself!

But what if you feel you can't or don't want to make a living from your passion? Does that make it any less of a passion in terms of how it can transform your life? I think not. Mother Teresa didn't work for pay. Does that mean she didn't have passion for what she did?

A passion is a passion because it's meaningful, not because it will make us rich or let us live on a beach for the rest of our days. What Tom didn't realize when his passion was asleep, was that the act of *participating* in his passion was exactly what he needed to build his own self-belief in what writing could do for his life.

There is something special about enacting a passion that unleashes power in each person. I do believe everyone can make a living from his or her passion. That's why I'm a big advocate that everyone should enact his or her passion. Even if the immediate rewards are not financial, the long-term pay-off is likely to be. Looking back on Tom's experience, I can see that Tom committed to acting on his passion the very first day he uncovered that passion. The result for him was stunning. But let's be clear. The personal power (self-belief) Tom gained from writing was not derived from what he wrote. It came from the fact that Tom was living his passion—and making it work.

PASSION NEEDS SPACE TO FLOURISH

Uncovering one's passion is a remarkable process. One of Tom's main access points to his passion was his emotion around family. Self-honesty was another. Rather than hold firmly to the perception of what a career in real estate would accomplish, Tom chose to explore the truth that he wasn't passionate about this work. Being open to the truth was a major aid to his growth. Tom readily admits this kind of honesty was not a common practice for him. So how did he do it this time?

Tom followed what I believe to be a proven approach to developing personal honesty. I've recommended this strategy to countless people, and it's the same approach I use myself. In fact, I use this technique whenever I start experiencing confusion, doubt, or extreme fear about any aspect of life.

I call it *taking* space. To put it into effect, you need to step away from all the tasks and busyness of life and spend time alone. Taking space is about your relationship with yourself, but it affects all areas of your life. Work and the passion (or lack of passion) you have for it is closely tied to your relationship with yourself, so improving your relationship with yourself will lead you to a better understanding and clarity around your work.

Taking space is magical. Until you start doing it regularly, you will have a hard time understanding the power of it. It removes all the external pressures and allows you to understand what the voice inside of you is saying. Many people haven't heard their internal voice in a long time, perhaps since they were children.

Taking space is a revelation to every person I've known who's actually done it. From the solitude, they suddenly realize they *do* have strong ideas about what they want out of life, and they gain more clarity than ever before. This is vital because we're constantly inundated with messages about what we *should* want out of life. This has the unexpected effect of leading us to ignore our internal guidance systems and allow others' wishes to rule over us.

Let's say, for example, that your spouse wants a bigger house. Their gentle desire might not initially bother us, but we may find over time that the voice becomes louder within us. It becomes a nagging nuisance. Before long, this idea can torture us, and it will affect everything we do.

On the job front, it means we don't have the option of quitting a job we hate, since that would stop us from buying the bigger house. Taking space may allow us to separate our spouse's desire from our own desire. We may find we don't want the house, and that we'd rather quit the job after all.

In another work-related scenario, your boss might want you to show up an hour earlier at the office every day to help him or her with a special project. This could interfere with your daily workout, which you do before work every morning.

You might do it because you don't want to upset your boss. Before long, you might forget you ever had a workout routine, and the lack of exercise might make you miserable. Taking space may allow you to see how you replaced your own desire with your boss's.

Failing to stay in tune with what you *really* want can impact other areas of your life, too. TV commercials, for example, might make you think your life is lacking if you don't lose 10 pounds, go on a vacation, buy a fancy car, or put your kids in the best private school. Taking space may allow you to see that everything is quite all right—and the only change you need is to stop watching the TV commercials.

Intellectually and emotionally, we are inundated with mixed messages about our choices from the moment we wake up until the moment we go to sleep. So much of this inundation is about what others want us to do, buy or be. These external messages can drown out our own small, simple, but consistent voices. That's right. We all have an inner voice that says, "This isn't it. There is something more fulfilling for me."

I'm convinced every person has this voice, no matter how quiet it might be for some of us. It will never stop speaking to us until the day we die, but we can only hear it by listening. But how do we listen to that voice? There's no better way than to create space, and then make a *habit* of taking that space. I prefer to take space in nature, but there are several ways to do it.

Some people love to meditate. Others love to exercise, go for a ride on their motorcycle, take a drive in their car or go for a walk.

While it's incredible to take a couple of days away, taking space doesn't have to involve a lot of time. I often advise people to start by taking just 30 minutes of space. If you work in an office, this might mean going for lunch by yourself in a park. For parents, it might mean taking the first 30 minutes after the kids go to bed to be alone.

We don't do this often enough. How many people working in an office rush off to eat lunch with the people they work with? And how many parents flick on the TV or start doing laundry the moment the kids go to bed?

Rather than taking space to be alone, most of us *run away* from alone time. We *run* into busyness by moving from task to task or we run towards a distraction such as TV, social media, emails or text messages.

There's a reason we keep ourselves busy. Many of us are scared we won't like the company of the person we find when we start taking space, so we avoid it. Being alone with one's self can be terrifying. I've counseled several clients to take space over the years, and many of them have reported being uncomfortable or even scared of being alone. Some people cannot even sit in a car on their own without the radio on.

But those who really give this technique a try typically end up making life-altering changes. I'm talking about people tripling their income, ending bad relationships or taking control of their health. For these people, listening to their inner voice was immensely powerful.

Taking space is a major part of my life. I can't imagine where I'd be without my regular ritual of taking space. Taking physical space is the first step that opens the way to create emotional and mental space in our lives. Create the space first, then allow the magic in.

THE POWER OF A FALSE BELIEF

"Perception is everything," is an oft-repeated saying in the training and personal growth industry.

There was a time when I fell into the perception trap, but I've come to see this belief as false—and dangerous. You may get by on perception for a while, but you end up living a lie if perception is your focus over truth. I spent a large portion of my youth living a lie. It's painful and debilitating.

Just as it takes effort to live your own personal truth, also it takes tremendous personal courage to *tell* your own truth. Tom is an example of the power of truth over perception. When I met him he was trying to maintain a perception as a "business guy" when, in reality, he was a writer. He was living a lie, but coming to his personal truth unlocked his inner strength.

When you're concerned with perception above personal truth, anxiety is guaranteed. That anxiety becomes a negative driving

force. Some of Tom's limiting beliefs were that:
- He needed to work in a traditional business
- He could not make money from writing
- He would be judged negatively by family and peers if he pursued writing
- He wouldn't be supported by family if he pursued his writing

Not one of these limiting beliefs helped Tom be the person he'd always wanted to be. But because he was acting on these false beliefs, the end result was an unauthentic and unhappy life.

Cleaning up our limiting beliefs is an ongoing process. Taking space is one very important step to identifying limiting beliefs, but it takes a great deal of *courage* to change those beliefs once they've been identified. And identifying them on your own can be difficult.

Limiting beliefs are a little easier to spot as they lie closer to the surface. There is another type of belief that I call "debilitating beliefs." Debilitating beliefs are subconscious hidden feelings that we generally don't think about.

Let's look at a few examples of the debilitating beliefs Tom held. Tom felt (not thought):

- I don't deserve to be a writer
- I don't deserve to make money doing something I love
- I don't deserve to be happy

It's debilitating beliefs like these that cripple peoples' lives and lead them to settle in life and have regrets. I love when the people I work with find courage to shatter perception, face their truth, and eliminate beliefs that don't serve them. The result of this process is authentic inner belief, the most powerful and beautiful force on earth.

You might remember that I once asked Tom what he wanted. His reply was, "to travel the world and write." As I write these words, he and his family are off travelling the world while he writes.

CONDITIONAL PASSION

One of the huge pressures we place on ourselves (and a sure way to crush it) is to make passion conditional. I recently met a young man who'd put his guitar away while pursuing financial freedom. His idea was to return to the guitar later, when he had the freedom to be able to play.

This is an insane approach to something that *feeds our soul*. One day he made an offhand remark to me that he played the guitar. I replied, "I didn't know you were a musician." He responded, "No, I'm not because I don't get an income from it."

Since when did money decide what makes a passion? If it's a passion you will do it for free. Money comes by following the passion.

Tom's example proves this to be true. While Tom took his time transitioning into writing, others move more quickly. The only thing that's for sure is that the only way to find out if we can make a living from our passion is to actually do it, do it consistently, and look for ways to integrate earning an income from our work.

Please don't make your passion conditional. Partake of whatever makes your soul burn. Kindle that little flame until it's a roaring fire. Don't let a lack of income stop you, especially when getting real with your own inner authenticity may well be the greatest business strategy you'll ever encounter.

CHAPTER 4:

AUTHENTICITY SELLS THE DEAL

"Fear is the assassin of dreams."
~ *Philip McKernan*

AUTHENTICITY AS BUSINESS STRATEGY

Have you ever made business or work decisions based on the belief that someone else could provide something you lack? Have those decisions ever led to an inauthentic feeling of following someone else's program or path?

This happens almost automatically and often without us even thinking about what's happening. But following others' programs, even when it seems practical and strategic, may not be a good thing if your soul is demanding you do something different. If you don't listen to it there will undoubtedly be some kind of fallout.

In this chapter, you'll see how honouring your intuition is the greatest way to develop authenticity, which is the ultimate business strategy and tool for a happy, fulfilled, and even materially-wealthy life. Authenticity has become the new currency.

A HEAVY HITTER

I was speaking at an event a couple of years back when I met a heavy hitter investment specialist named Steve. At the end of my talk, he approached me, saying there was much on his mind and he needed some guidance. I eventually ended up working with him in more detail. But on that day, our discussion was intense.

Steve was doing well in business, yet he had a sense something wasn't quite right. He explained how he and his business partner had been successful together. I got the sense there was something about the partnership Steve was uneasy about. Upon further questioning, Steve admitted something was amiss within the partnership, and he didn't know what his next step would be.

He explained it to me like this: although he had business success, Steve realized there was a disconnection between the ambitions and goals of the business and his own personal desire for a more fulfilling lifestyle. Part of that disconnection was caused by the different goals of his partner.

On one hand, Steve loved the thrill of business. He liked the income his business produced, and he enjoyed building businesses. On the other hand, Steve also longed for a more relaxing lifestyle that didn't demand he work every day from 5 a.m. until 8 p.m.

Once a physically healthy man, Steve's fitness level was no longer where he wanted it to be. He loved outdoor pursuits like mountain biking, motorcycling, and skiing, but a burdensome workload prevented him from pursuing those activities as much as he wanted.

A business veteran, Steve was no longer intimidated by the

prospect of a new business deal. This gave him a certain confidence. He knew he could accomplish whatever he wanted in business and that he could capitalize on opportunities because he had the knowledge, team, and reputation to execute. What was missing was desire. Steve didn't necessarily *want* to capitalize on new deals simply because they were there.

He also told me he felt pulled in different directions, and not always in directions he necessarily wanted to go. The problem centred around his business partner and their differing visions for the company. Whereas Steve sought life fulfillment and a business that supported that lifestyle, the partner wanted to grow the company rapidly. He appeared to be unaware of the cost to his own lifestyle and health.

Steve admitted he could be enthusiastic about the possibilities for growth. But he also knew there was a disconnect between him and his partner. He was aware of his heart's longing for peace of mind and well-being, and he knew his hectic work schedule had already exacted a physical, mental and emotional cost.

Steve eventually told me he wanted to part ways with the business partner, but he was concerned his investments would suffer. Why? Because Steve thought it was the partner who drew investors to the business. Despite this fear, Steve was convinced he needed to make the change.

After a number of conversations, Steve made the move and broke the news to the partner that the partnership was ending. It was not easy, but he felt it was the best thing to do.

The timing of Steve's decision was purposeful because he had an investor meeting scheduled for a week later. He knew he'd have to tell the investors about the breakup of the partnership during that meeting.

Steve told me he wasn't sure how he would do this. He knew he wasn't going to betray his former partner by saying anything negative about him. But he needed to tell the investors the partnership was over, that he was moving forward, and that he wanted the investors to move forward with him. He feared that many of the investors would walk away from him and that they were only there because of the partner in the first place.

When the day came to speak to the investors, Steve went up to the front of the room and described his feelings around the partnership, how there was a professional incongruence, and how he'd terminated the partnership.

Steve went on to explain how it was important that his personal values matched up with his business, and he felt that there was a chasm between what he felt in his heart and what he experienced in his business. He told the investors he was certain working with a partner whose goals and aspirations were different caused the rift.

He was careful not to say anything negative about the former partner. Instead, he told the investors the partnership needed to end because it wasn't right. He also explained how he was still going forward as the lead on his current investment project. The result shocked him.

Typically, it would take six to eight months to sell out a project like the one Steve was working on. He was stunned when the *entire* investment sold out that night! Not only that, the investors wanted more. They were asking him when his next project would be available.

One of the biggest money investors took Steve aside and explained that up to that night he'd been concerned about investing in the company. Steve's presentation changed that. The investor put a significant amount of money into the project and brought another big money player with him.

Telling the investors the simple, unadorned, vulnerable truth yielded jaw-dropping results. Steve had never witnessed such a phenomenon in his career.

FACING HIS TRUTH

I wouldn't say that all partnerships are negative. But there is a common thread that runs through many partnerships. We often want to join with another partner because we don't feel we could be as successful on our own as we could with a partner.

Entrepreneurs will bring someone else on board because of a perceived lack in their own business. In Chapter 2, Tara believed she couldn't do the marketing and build internal business systems to support the growth she wanted for her business. In truth, Tara could have solved those issues by hiring specialists. She did not have to give away a large portion of her business to achieve her business goals.

Steve was much the same. He started his investment company and brought in a partner whom he perceived would be vastly superior at bringing investors and attracting money. Steve thought that would give him time to focus on analysis and asset acquisition.

Since Steve liked some of his partner's ideas for expansion, he began to think his partner was more ambitious than him. Steve didn't like the lifestyle his business partner's approach promoted, but he thought he was powerless to change it. Whenever we bring a partner into our business, there's a strong possibility we'll have the following realizations:

1.   We find out the partner is not as great as we thought
2.   We find out we can do more than we thought

In my business experience, and in working with hundreds of entrepreneurs, these two realizations happen in many partnerships. This doesn't necessarily mean every partnership is bad, but it does put partnerships into a new perspective.

Steve's decision to evaluate the partnership and then tell investors about his new (partner-less) approach was the direct result of getting in touch with his truth. This illustrates why I see the truth is everything—and perception is nothing. The moment Steve stepped into his truth and fully owned it, he found he didn't have any problem raising money. That was the exact opposite of his perception.

When we *need* something desperately, we tend to ignore the intuitive signs of our own internal guidance system. This is what Steve was doing before he ended the partnership. Telling the investors the truth unleashed a powerful force. But before he got up in front of the investors, Steve had fearful thoughts about what the investors might do. He thought and planned and strategized about how he was going to present and position the breakup.

In the end, it was the simple truth that freed him from his concerns, and unlocked enormous trust for him as well as investment money in his project.

SCARED OF THE TRUTH

Inside each person resides a core that remains unchanged by the opinions and beliefs of others. Experience has shown me that we all know what's inside. However, we're often too scared to face that truth and be fully authentic with it.

But, we *must* tap into this core to find our power in the world. The more logical, mind-driven of us may think this is airy-fairy, but I promise you, we each have an internal guidance system. At our own peril, we fail to listen to it. In addition to that internal core, which does speak to us if we give it a chance, there are also hundreds, thousands, possibly millions of other voices we hear. But, those voices aren't ours. Other people, circumstances, and events plant them within. We've given those voices more power in our lives than the one little voice that matters most—our own.

Most of us have one or several voices within that say, "You're not good enough, you don't deserve this," and so on. The voice that haunted me for most of my life said, "Who the fuck is going to listen to you?"

Deep inside, Steve didn't believe he could run his business as well by himself as he could with his partner. When he stepped into that truth with his actions, he was able to see just how powerful he was, how his own voice was a better guide than the other voices. Why was Steve afraid of the truth?

LIVING IN YOUR HEAD

In my short e-book, *Dead Man Walking*, I discussed the difference between mindset and soulset. My experience has proven that our intellect is a powerful ability, but it can also be a crutch.

In that book, I discussed how people have a deep ability to be intuitive, which is powerful but rarely used today. Some of the most creative and intelligent people who've ever lived agree with me, too. Notably, Albert Einstein and Steve Jobs were huge proponents and practitioners of the intuitive ability.

"The intuitive mind is a sacred gift and the rational mind is a faithful servant. We have created a society that honours the servant and has forgotten the gift."
~ *Albert Einstein*

I actually believe that our intuition *can't* be wrong, but I'm certainly not in the majority with my belief. Our intuition is always at work, yet we don't follow its advice because of our total belief in the value of intellect.

This disconnect leads us to make decisions based on the wrong reasons, thus producing results we'll never be happy with. It's the reason so many people reach a goal and then feel no joy or contentment. Our goals are produced in our minds, while our gut wants something different. Results are stunning when the intellect is made the faithful servant of intuition.

Reconnecting to intuition is one of the most powerful things we can do to promote positive change in our lives. Steve is a perfect example. Eventually things got to the point where even though he knew intuitively that something was wrong with his partnership, he couldn't put his finger on was the problem was intellectually. Prior to listening to his intuition, he had no shortage of logical reasons why he needed to remain in the partnership. Following his intuition, and then speaking his truth, he saw real power unlocked in his life.

Many (if not most) of us neglect our intuition. It might even seem to us that we don't have intuition. But just as grass is healthier when we water and apply fertilizer, our intuition is healthier when we nurture it. Steady neglect obviously weakens our intuition. But why do we neglect our intuition?

We start neglecting it the moment someone tells us we're wrong as a child. We start when we tell someone we want to be a professional snowboarder—and they tell us to stop dreaming and think about getting a real job. It happens in "our best interest." Others' voices simply have too much of an impact upon us from a young age and these voices crush our intuition.

Steve, like most people, had been ignoring his intuition for a long time. Once he started listening to it, he and his investors benefitted enormously.

STRONG EMOTIONAL BLOCKS TO INTUITION

Some of the emotions we experience act as powerful detractors of our intuition. For example, fear drives people into their heads and away from what they know is right in their soul.

Anger can make people delusional. They fail to see reality coherently when anger takes over. Most people are angry, but very few are aware of it or willing to see it, which makes the anger even more destructive. Instead of recognizing anger as an emotional response created by your story, society tells us it is something to be ashamed of.

Strong emotions take hold of our thoughts and twist them in such a way that reality becomes perception versus truth. Steve was afraid he couldn't attract investors on his own. This feeling blocked the intuition that was screaming at him to ditch the partner. Unable to hear his own inner voice, Steve turned to his intellect and sought the answer there.

We pride ourselves on being clever. It's clever to invite a successful partner into our business. It's clever to find people to fill the gaps in our own perceived weaknesses. It's clever to be "realistic" about what we can and can't do.

But honouring our own truth, following our intuition, and doing exactly what's right for our personal journey isn't clever. It's courageous. Doing what we know is right in our core takes enormous courage. It means overcoming our fear and anger. It means deeply trusting ourselves.

I can understand why people run from their truths and ignore their intuition. Facing up to our truth and following our intuition is scary. It involves risk because it sometimes means doing what doesn't make logical or practical sense. We start to hear niggling little voices, which can overtake us and flood us with fear. What if I'm wrong? What if I'm not good enough? What if I can't do it?

These questions, and many more like them, will plague us and taunt us. They will push us into our heads and force us to devise clever plans that circumvent our intuition with intellect. But all the clever plans in the world can never quiet the voices screaming at us that we're wrong. On the contrary, the more we yield to the voices of doubt and the more we seek solace from the doubts in our clever plans, the more we find ourselves adrift from our core being.

I advocate that people come back to their truth by listening to their intuition. When we get out of our heads and into our souls, there's a conviction to be found. No amount of dollars, and nobody else's apparent talents, will allow us to waiver from that place.

But when fear, anger, or others' voices of doubt push us back into our heads, we lose our intuitive sense of direction. We become like sheep, looking for the next shepherd to lead us somewhere "better."

SEEING THE PATTERN

For Steve, the result of listening to his intuition was stunning. He never would've imagined that he could attract the investment money he did, nor that his intuition would lead him to peace of mind.

While I focused this discussion on one issue in Steve's business life, situations like this rarely show up in isolation. If it was happening in Steve's business life, there's every chance it was happening in other areas as well.

That's because problems never happen in isolation. Problems begin in one place and spread. After they identify one crack in their lives, people often think they can build a firewall around that one area and keep the problem from infecting other aspects of their lives. Once Steve opened up to working on his partnership issue, we found other cracks that he also needed to face.

My experience with Steve is not isolated. All of us put on masks for our daily business life, masks for our home life, masks for our parents, and masks for our friends. While we're still the same person underneath the masks, these disguises help us hide from others and ourselves!

DEVELOP A SOULSET

Your intuition isn't wrong now, has never been wrong, and (here's the great news) will never be wrong. The challenge then becomes, can we turn off the noise and truly hear it?

You may not know how to interpret what your intuition is telling you, but I encourage you to accept that your intuition is never wrong. I'm not saying that our intellect doesn't have value. On the contrary, the intellect is an incredibly powerful tool that, when put in its right place, can be used to create immense change and growth.

But putting the intellect in its right place demands development of what I call a soulset. Personal development and success literature puts a lot of emphasis on mindset. Fair enough. But mindset is nothing unless it serves soulset.

Those who take space to hear what their intuition tells them will learn to take action on that intuition. Over time, these people will develop soulset. Steve's story is not a simple story of a guy who had the wrong partner in business. It's the story of a man who, for a time, had given up the most important partnership in the world—the partnership he had with himself.

> *"I totally regret listening to my gut - Said no one ever."*
> *~ Oliver Manalese*

CHAPTER 5:

FROM MONEY MAGNATE TO CHILDREN'S CHAMPION

"If you're facing the right direction, all you need to do is walk."
~ *Philip McKernan*

ATTACHMENT BLOCKS FULFILLMENT

Have you ever wanted something so bad that the thought of not achieving it is almost painful? Have you ever taken extreme measures in the quest of this desire?

In the last chapter we talked about how authenticity and soulset lead us to more fulfillment and happiness. Taking what we learned in that chapter, I want to talk about how our attachment to certain achievements blocks us from living authentically, developing a soulset, and therefore ultimately finding more meaning and its resulting by-product, happiness.

THE INVESTOR

When I met Trina, her daughter was just starting university. That meant Trina was entering her empty nest years. This was, for

Trina, a time of change. She didn't know exactly what that change entailed, but she had decided to pursue some aggressive business goals during this time.

Trina owned a gorgeous home, a stable full of horses, and a bunch of real estate properties. The home and horses fuelled her personal pleasures, and the real estate was her business venture.

Trina saw her home and horses as the fulfillment of a lifelong dream to own a beautiful home in the country with a large stable full of horses. She was thrilled with her possessions, but felt something was missing.

In particular, Trina was spending more of her time with the real estate investments than inside her grand home or with her horses. Financially speaking, the real estate investments were working out well. Still, Trina was somewhat unsure of where to turn next. Hoping to figure out the next step she hired a business coach.

Like many consultants and business coaches, Trina's business coach was fantastic at taking what she'd created and helping her develop a plan for future growth. Together they devised a strategy and a marketing platform for her to leverage her real estate holdings into an empire.

Backed by a plan, Trina employed strategies to raise money from investors, and acquire new real estate assets. She also started branding herself as the leading authority in her niche market.

Trina came to me at about the same time she was developing her brand. While I understood her decision to seek additional guidance, I was hesitant. It's often awkward to work with entrepreneurs who are also working with another consultant or coach.

Before starting, I spoke with Trina a number of times. After listening to her story, and after some soul-searching on my part, I believed I could be of assistance to her. Following my own approach to authenticity, intuition and soulset, I asked Trina to question every aspect of her life, including the brand she was developing. This process took several months. In the early days, Trina was fully on board with her new brand and thought she was on the best business path for her. Over time, a different picture began to develop.

Trusting my intuition, I continued to poke around this idea. Something wasn't right, and I questioned her about it. She continued to affirm her excitement for the branding process. One day our discussion about her business included the fact she'd hired a blogger in India to create content and write posts on her social media accounts. Trina also mentioned that she didn't really like the content. In fact, she felt totally disconnected from its message.

The doubts she expressed to me about the blogging content were the first opening she provided that perhaps the branding strategy wasn't for Trina, an authentic choice. I soon noticed an emerging pattern. Each time Trina met with her business consultant, she was effectively re-attached to this branding strategy. This was problematic in that it appeared to show that Trina's business consultant—and not Trina—was driving the plan.

This went on for some months. Trina waffled on the branding strategy, then got reattached after talking to her consultant. Every time I asked her to tell me what her soul was telling her, Trina released some of that attachment.

Little-by-little, more cracks started showing up. We spoke about the reasons she wanted to follow the strategy and how it made her feel. We spoke about how authentic it was, and we questioned why she was attached to this version of success.

These conversations helped Trina recognize that she needed to put her intellect in service of her intuition. In all of the work I've done, I don't think this conflict between mind and soul has ever been more apparent to me than it was within Trina.

From a logical perspective, it made perfect sense for Trina to pursue this branding strategy. But it wasn't in her heart, and it became obvious that Trina was resisting the branding strategy on a level she didn't understand. In fact, her lack of heart connection to the branding strategy was the reason she'd hired me as her personal coach. I don't think either of us knew this at the time, although my own commitment to intuition meant I was sure something like this was going on!

Trina was torn between her intellect and her intuition. But she came to realize the branding strategy didn't represent what was in her soul, and that she'd have to let it go. While this led to some uncertainty about what was next, it wasn't long before Trina figured that out.

The crux of the problem was that the branding strategy focused solely on the intellectual side of Trina's business. The plan served her intellectual desire. Unfortunately, that put her heart's desire at risk.

When your intuition senses something is not quite right, its often easier to stay on the current course that you think logically is clear, as opposed to changing course based on a feeling that often has no clear logical direction. This is were the trust you have in yourself comes in.

As humans we talk a lot about trusting others, while I believe the most important person to learn to trust, is you.

CREATE SPACE TO LET THE MAGIC IN

It took some time, but Trina eventually let go of the attachment to the real estate niche branding strategy. With that no longer cluttering her intellectual space, she spent some time contemplating what the next step was. I know this was difficult for Trina. It's difficult for anyone, especially driven business people who are accustomed to knowing exactly what's next at all times.

A couple of months later, I received an excited phone call from Trina. While driving down the road the day before, she heard a radio ad for a private academy franchise. "It was as though I'd been hit by a bolt of lightning, Philip. I felt electric."

Suddenly, her professional journey made perfect sense. She *loved* working with children. She *loved* teaching and always had. When she heard the ad, it became apparent to her that there was a viable business model for teaching kids. She decided on the spot that she'd buy the rights to one of the franchises. The intuitive truth was so obvious that it prompted Trina to move quickly. About two months later, she was the proud owner of a tutoring franchise.

The shift from intellect to intuition enabled Trina to let go of her feigned passion for a business venture she wasn't at all passionate about. Trina doesn't have to fake anything when helping kids. She loved it, and the passion showed.

Trina recently sent me an email about a boy who was put into remedial math in high school. After a summer of tutoring at Trina's school, he improved dramatically. When he showed up in class and took the first assessment test, the teacher immediately took the boy aside and said, "Why are you in this class? You're way beyond this level."

But the move to a regular class was just the start. In his new higher-level class, the young man worked hard. By finishing all of his extra assignments and his regular daily work, he'd achieved a grade of 106%[1] in the first semester.

This was one of Trina's proudest accomplishments. Trina's email told me how much this meant to her, how fulfilled she was, and how proud she was of the work she was doing. The change in the confidence of these young people was a bigger reward than she could imagine.

THE STORY BEHIND THE STORY: ATTACHMENTS

When Trina and I delved into her personal story, we found that many of her supposed drives were unauthentic. Rather than being inspired by real estate, Trina was holding onto an attachment around the traditionally-received notion of success. Unfortunately, this wasn't serving her authentic self.

The business consultant played into that attachment by helping Trina pursue a version of success that appeared so logical it failed to ask Trina if that's what she even *wanted* to do.

Business coaches can be valuable for entrepreneurs. I don't

---

[1] Extra credit was earned resulting in a grade above 100% by completing extra assignments.

question that. The strategies they devise can help entrepreneurs launch or expand a business. But the traditional business consultant typically leaves out a couple of very important questions and considerations.

- *Why* would Trina want to become a real estate mogul?
- Why would she want to brand herself aggressively in a business she didn't own at the core?

As it turned out, Trina's real interest in real estate was caught up in what I call the *standard version of success*. It had no relation to what her soul desired.

The standard version of success is about money, numbers, and proving oneself to others (family members, old friends, society). Some people are so attached to proving themselves to others that they continue on this path even after the people they're trying to impress have passed away.

Without an authentic answer as to *why*, our stated desire for success will always be mired in standardly received notions. Trina did not have a deep why for the real estate business. This is why the cracks eventually showed up.

What do I really want? That's one of the most powerful questions we can possibly ask ourselves. It's also one few consultants ever ask since their main focus is to take what you bring them, and then multiply it by two, three, five, or ten. That's fine, but at what cost? What is the trade off? What is the social invoice?

For Trina, the opportunity to take space, while stepping back from a business strategy that made her uncomfortable, gave her the opportunity to open herself up to another business venture. I do not believe she could have made such a passionate transformation without first letting go of the initial attachment she had to her new marketing strategy. Once she let go of that attachment, she saw that its intellectual value was not in tune with her intuition.

Before we leave Trina's story, we should ask ourselves why she was so attached to a traditional version of success. This attachment is obviously at the root of why she brought a consultant into her life in the first place. While the answers are fundamentally unique to each person, it's important that we don't discount the fact that Trina was obviously attempting to set goals for her personal and business life.

THE PROBLEM WITH ATTACHMENTS

Goal setting is generally seen as a positive, even necessary, process. One frequently-reported Harvard statistic notes that only 3% of people have written-down goals. Based on a focus group in the late 1970s, this same statistic claimed that 10 years later that goal-setting cohort was earning 10-times more than the other 97%. The unspoken message is that the 3% with higher earnings were the 3% who also set goals and wrote them down.

But did this study not look at engagement, happiness, fulfillment or quality of health levels, let alone peace of mind? It focused only on the traditionally received version of success: money.

I have a different perspective on goals. I believe a goal is usually just an attachment made official. When we set a goal, it's as though we're officially saying to the world, "Here's my attachment, and I intend to do whatever it takes to achieve the object of my attachment."

People want change, growth, and success, but they don't realize the pressure they put themselves under to reach change, growth, and success. The attachment most people have to reaching goals is enormous and crushing.

For example, I see people attached to goals that are fundamentally unhealthy. I see them maintain attachments even as their key relationships, including marriages, fall apart. I see people attached to goals that directly cost them the opportunity to participate in and appreciate their children's youth. Instead of seeing what's real, good, and right, they are blinded by goals that, in hindsight, will not matter at all.

This pursuit of goals leads many people to use visualization as a method for achieving their goals. These individuals believe visualizing a goal in excruciating detail (colour, shape, taste, you name it!) will cause that goal, typically in the shape of an object, to appear.

To me, this practice sounds like a how-to manual for developing unhealthy attachments—and disappointment.

People even use this method when seeking love. Imagine a man wants to find the perfect woman. He imagines what she will look like down to the size of her breasts, the colour of her hair and eyes, the length of her hair, her height, her build, her weight, her profession, and how she dresses.

He imagines *everything* about her, including the place where they'll meet. If he envisions meeting her in a particular upscale lounge in a stylish part of town, he'll even go to that lounge on a specific night.

Individuals who fall into traps like this might sit in that lounge and stare at the door for hours, just waiting for the perfect girl to walk in. By the time he goes home he'll be demoralized that his visualizing exercise didn't work.

A client of mine went on a blind date recently and it became mutually obvious that there was simply no connection between them. It was then that the games stopped and the masks were removed and the conversation deepened.

When my client was getting ready for the evening she found herself putting on make up and perfume that is not really her. In fact, she never wears perfume and prefers a more natural look. In the now authentic conversation later in the evening, the man she had met on the blind date expressed how he prefers women who don't wear too much makeup, or wear perfume.

Thinking back to Trina's situation, it wasn't as though she didn't already know that she loved teaching and helping children. She was unable to see this as a pursuable (and worthy) passion because she was so attached to the standard version of success. In sum, Trina was blinded by her attachments. And that's the problem with all attachments. Because they don't allow us to see beyond them, we miss out on much of the beauty and potential in life.

To those who say they cannot make a living doing something they love, I have a one-word response: bullshit.

> *"Once you become blinded by attachments*
> *you become deaf to your heart."*
> *~ Philip McKernan*

WHERE ELSE?

Trina was thrilled with her transition away from real estate and towards a career helping and inspiring kids through her tutoring business. Her life was now on the path she'd always hoped it would be. She was deeply engaged in a rewarding business—and having the time of her life doing it.

This experience with intuition and authenticity eventually informed other parts of Trina's life. She even thought of her large and wonderful home differently. Through much self-reflection, Trina realized she was attached to that home in much the same way she'd once been attached to real estate.

Trusting what she'd learned from listening to her own intuition, Trina sold her house and moved into a much more modest home. That decision dramatically reduced the financial stress caring for that home was causing. In addition to the financial worry, the home demanded much of her energy. She was either caring for the grounds herself or constantly hiring others to do it.

Trina was a bit surprised that she didn't miss the house at all. The last time I spoke to her about this change, she told me she was thrilled to have simplified her life.

By this point, Trina was on a mission to identify—and authentically deal—with all of her attachments. After the house, she turned her attention to her horses. The sale of one precious horse brought such relief she's considering selling them all. It's not that Trina doesn't love her horses. What she has discovered is that she loves herself, too.

Trina's story illustrates the need to question what we bring into our lives. I'm not against people having wonderful things like horses and big homes. But all of us should question our attachments. Once Trina went down this path, she discovered that removing certain attachments allowed her to be happier.

Now that she's removed these attachments from her life with such beautiful precision, Trina sees that she is control of what gets added. Knowing the difference between an attachment and a true passion, she can look beyond standard versions of success.

OPENNESS

When I met Trina, she also wanted to meet a man and start a relationship. As of the time of writing this, she had not yet started that relationship, but great things happen with time. Perhaps a man she loves will come into her life in the same way her business did, like a bolt of lightning.

What I can say for certain is that she's in a far better place to meet a great man than she was when she was attached to the standard version of success.

The rather simple truth of relationships is that we get exactly what we put out into the world. When we put out an unauthentic version of ourselves, we end up with an unauthentic version of a partner.

This is true in my own life. It is not a coincidence that I met my wife, Pauline, in South America. Traveling is one of my favourite activities, and South America is a place I love deeply. As I am truly myself when there, I'm not surprised it's where I met the love of my life and future wife.

It's simple. Love yourself and do what makes you happy, and

you'll be more likely to find someone attracted to that energy.

My advice to anyone looking for an authentic, life-long relationship is to let that attachment go and work on the things you can control. Then live your life fully and trust that the right person will show up. This might mean removing from your vision board the photo of Pamela Anderson or Brad Pitt. But the sooner you let go of attachments that are outside your control, the happier you'll be.

In fact, once you accept how devastating attachments can be to living authentically and to having authentic business success, you'll see how quickly decisions can be made—and business fulfillment achieved. I see it with my clients all the time. This is where you'll see how releasing attachments opens our minds to see the truth of our existence.

This focus on the work side of our existence is important because work is one of the three major elements of life. Now we'll move on to the most important relationship we have; the relationship with ourselves.

NOW, LET'S BRING IT HOME

<u>Before</u> you turn to the next section, please grab a journal and take some real time to answer these questions. Take your time on these.

1. Do you suffer from the Next Level Syndrome? Why?
2. Do you put people on a pedestal? Who?
3. Are you passionate or are you excited about the work you do?
4. What is the negative voice inside your head saying?
5. Guaranteed you could not fail, what work would you choose

to do?

6. Make a list of five things you are attached to in your life. Then ask a) why and b) do they serve you?

PART TWO:
SELF

YOUR RELATIONSHIP TO WHO YOU ARE

"Success is manufactured in the mind,
while happiness is cultivated in the soul."
~ Philip McKernan

THE ORIGINAL RELATIONSHIP

People unfamiliar with my work are often surprised when I refer to the self-relationship as a key relationship. For the purpose of in-person mentoring, I often use the lenses of Work, Self, and Others to stimulate thought and deepen awareness.

My belief is that it's these three areas of life where we spend the bulk of our time (and effort). It's also the areas where change can make the biggest impact. By creating or deepening the meaning we derive in each of these three elements, a greater degree of happiness is available.

The idea that we have a relationship with work and other people doesn't surprise anyone. But few of us contemplate the very real relationship we have with ourselves. If you're someone who thinks this way, I'd like you to think about your response to words you hear inside your own head. More specifically, to whom do you think that voice is speaking?

Our self-relationship is our most important relationship. While the relationship we have to a spouse or partner is our most important external relationship, it cannot supersede our self-relationship. As you read through the following stories about self-relationships, please take the time to reflect on your own self-relationship. Do you even think of your self-relationship? What kinds of things do you say to yourself?

CHAPTER 6:

THE BAD MOTHER

"It's generally the things we don't do that haunt us forever."
~ Philip McKernan

HOW WE REALLY THINK OF OURSELVES

Laura approached me after hearing me speak at an event in Calgary. She's the mother of two children, a boy in his early twenties and a girl in her early teens. Each of the kids has a different father from a different marriage.

Laura faced some difficult and harsh circumstances during her two marriages. She worked through the hard times and emerged as a successful, independent woman and a dedicated mother.

When I met her, however, she fundamentally believed she was a bad mother. She didn't use those words exactly, but I knew that's how she felt deep down. Laura's relationship with her son was a big cause of this belief. She knew he was making dangerous choices and putting himself in physical risk. She didn't have good communication with him, which exacerbated how painful and scary his behaviour was for Laura.

As a result of our interaction, Laura told me that she believed her son's life direction was her fault. Because she'd been divorced twice, she thought she'd failed to provide her son with a happy home to grow up in. Because his early years were not spent in a traditional family environment, Laura carried immense guilt about her self-perceived lack.

That guilt was manifested in the perception that Laura was broken as a person and as a mother. Still, Laura wasn't about to give up. She knew that she and her son deserved better, so she sought change.

LAURA'S DREAM TRIP

As with many people, Laura had a dream that she thought would improve her life. She always wanted to live part of the year in Italy, and she wanted to bring her kids.

She worked hard, saved money, and planned the trip in her mind. A couple of years ago, Laura was finally able to make the trip. She and her kids left on a month-long journey to explore Italy and its culture.

The trip turned out to be significant for the family. The space provided by spending a whole month together so far from home allowed Laura the space to be vulnerable with her kids. Recognizing the trip as a special opportunity, Laura had done some self-work in advance. Once in Italy, their opportunity to talk presented itself. Instead of falling into past patterns where she might have lectured her son about the choices he was making, Laura changed the content and tone of her message. Using simple words like, "I messed up" and "I'm sorry" she gave her son a chance to talk, too. Laura really *listened* to her son. This turned out to be the most important action she could take.

Rather than lecturing him about the choices he was making, Laura simply told him the truth about how she felt, then listened to him respond. These simple changes led to rapid transformation of the family dynamic and the relationships they shared.

I agree that you can't change other people. But if you set out to change yourself, and then invite others to come along, changing others is inevitable. People follow examples.

Personal transformation is available when we peel layer by layer to our truest self and when we have the guts to carry out our dreams. Laura's first journey to Italy with her kids is a perfect example of how this works.

THE NEXT PHASE

A couple of years later, Laura embarked upon another journey. But this time she went by herself. Isn't it interesting how our physical journeys often correlate with our internal journeys?

This time Laura went to Ireland on a journey of self-discovery. Along with a small group of seekers, she spent a week in a tiny fishing village on Ireland's west coast to participate in an annual retreat I run there.

The experience is about getting away from the world, getting out of our heads, connecting with nature, exploring ancient culture, and allowing the clarity to emerge from within from an intuitive place. Laura left Ireland at the end of the retreat with further growth and renewed insight. On top that, she *had fun* in Ireland.

At the end of the retreat, with several new friendships, powerful insights, and memories she'll never forget, Laura went back to Italy to fulfill another dream. On the first trip there, she reconnected with her kids. On this second trip, she was looking for more insight into herself and clarity around living in Italy.

By the way, this kind of purposeful travel is available to all of us to reconnect to ourselves. The problem is that most people travel to *get away* from themselves, their lives and their work. Laura and other self-aware people travel to *be with* themselves.

Do you see the difference? Laura knew the difference, and she had something more important—openness. Because she was open, Laura discovered an incredible thing in Italy. She preferred Ireland! What?

When I spoke to her after she returned from Italy, Laura reported that in Ireland she met people and had a blast everywhere she went. But in Italy, she never managed to start a conversation with strangers. Before you dismiss it as the language barrier, think of it this way.

After the experience, Laura realized that her attraction to Italy was based on the same false assumptions as one's attraction to the cool kids in school. Even if you really want to hang out with this crowd, it's not one you're comfortable with.

Ireland, on the other hand, represented a more authentic relationship. It gave her the chance to spend time with the kind of people she valued. The people she met in Ireland are easy to get along with, easy to meet, and easy to laugh with. Laura even felt she could dress the way she wanted without the pressure.

Here's the thing. Laura wasn't saying all people in Italy are snobs or all Irish people are friendly. The two visits to two different countries back-to-back were just emblematic of an internal process. It was less about the countries, and more about her allowing herself to be authentic with whom she is at the core.

In spite of the amazing first trip to Italy, the second trip, along with the stopover in Ireland, was an eye opener because it helped Laura shine a light within. She knew what she really wanted, not only from a country where she was visiting, but also from herself.

Laura realized Italy represented something she felt she wanted to be, while Ireland was all about being herself. The contrasting experiences of Italy and Ireland helped Laura illuminate another personal idiosyncrasy. It helped her draw a line that enabled better self-understanding.

Laura is an interior designer and has achieved great success. Sometimes people unfamiliar with the profession will refer to her as an interior decorator. It's an honest mistake made by people who don't know the difference, but Laura *hated* being called an interior decorator. She felt it minimized her professional role. What the error really did was challenge her self-identity.

Just as Laura perceived Italy to be a premium location, she believed that interior design represented premium profession. Anything less, on either front, was second rate. In reality, it all came down to her desire to attach herself to status symbols in order to fit in. After Ireland, Laura questioned her admiration of all-things-Italian and began wondering why she was so attached to the interior designer label. While Laura's journey is far from over, her self-discoveries have changed the way she sees—and experiences—the world.

LISTENING TO EGO OVER HEART

I believe the heart of every individual longs for the same thing—to love and be loved. In Laura's case, she felt her ability to love and give love had been compromised. Because she considered herself broken, she felt she couldn't give or receive love.

What Laura discovered through getting to know and appreciate herself, was that she wasn't broken. As realizations go, this was powerful. But the transformation didn't stop there. An authentic understanding of who she was and what she offered the world led Laura to realize she had developed a deeply held desire to help children.

I've seen this kind of transformation several times when individuals believe they're not capable of giving love—and then realize they want to be of service to the world by helping children. To Laura, it was an epiphany.

I do know that Laura wouldn't have discovered this facet of herself without first understanding more about who she is and learning to communicate with her own children. To Laura, it was a discovery. From my perspective, it was a re-discovery. While Laura didn't know this part of herself, I believe it was there from the start! Why was this aspect of who she is shut off from Laura? Because she, like many of us, had shut herself off from her soul's desires. When we do that, we don't just lose the ability to hear ourselves, we lose the ability to heal ourselves.

The basic problem is that we live in a world of disconnection. Most people don't know what they truly want, let alone what they want to do, or whom they want to serve. This statement has been verified by hundreds of personal experiments within my own work. Clients often tell me about their elaborate plans for business or personal growth, and when I push them a little bit to explain why they have chosen a particular path, their answers are often an elaborately-crafted justification for why they can't do the things they really want to do. That's unfortunate. The ego wins the day; the heart retreats a little further into the corner.

It's normal to feel internal conflict between what we think we should do and what we really want to do. It's normal to want to fit in with the cool kids in school, drive the nicest car, and travel to the sexiest locations. This comes from a basic desire that says we are "better" when other people envy us. It judges success against an imaginary *better person* or *better version* of ourselves.

This powerful force is all about the ego. The ego wants to fit in, and it'll crush what the heart desires in return for pursuing what it *thinks* the heart should desire. Laura's ego made her believe she'd failed as a parent and believed that living in Italy would add meaning to her life. All she really wanted was authentic relationships with her kids and herself! The non-ego force within us speaks far more quietly. It knows when something is right regardless what others might think. It wants to help others; it wants to create. It smiles, it radiates, and it glows. I'm speaking of our heart's desire, our soul's longing. It's a beautiful concept if you allow it in.

> *"Listen to your heart and then take action to honour your soul."*
> ~ *Philip McKernan*

WHAT'S IN A NAME?

When Ireland joined the eurozone, I recall having meaningful conversations with my countrymen who disagreed with me when I said Ireland risked losing itself in the much larger stream of

Europe. Ultimately, I thought that while there may be economic advantages to joining the eurozone, there would also be a cost. More specifically, I believed it would result in the dilution of our core culture. The people I argued with contended that Ireland's strong culture meant we'd never lose our identity.

Both points had some validity. But there's no question Ireland has lost some of its identity. Post euro, there is a broad sense that Ireland is just one cog in the larger European wheel.

I believe that Ireland's experience mirrors what happens when individuals make compromises about how they choose to self-identify. Never before has humanity more needed a place to call home, something to believe in, and something to feel part of. As many of the heroes and institutions we've historically held in high regard falter, people feel more isolated and insecure than ever.

When a country chooses a path based on economic security and prosperity, it is rewarded with jobs, new roads, a strong currency, more exports, and a great sense of wealth. Similarly, national choices about cultural security promote the kind of prosperity linked to shared identity and pride.

At a more personal level, I believe many women experience a kind of identity crisis related to changing their family names when they get married. My own wife chose to change her name to McKernan when we were married. I am honoured by her choice. But as someone fundamentally concerned with ideas related to self-identity, I think it's worth asking what a woman "gives up" when she makes this choice. At the very least, changing one's surname changes the individual's link to their own past history.

Adding children to the mix often presents another life-altering shift in self-identification. While children are a beautiful gift, and we learn so much from them, there's no doubt that many parents (and mothers in particular) radically alter their self-identification once children enter the picture. This happens because your life is suddenly focused more on what you do as opposed to who you are. I've seen this in clients enough times to know this is a common issue.

Harkening back to Laura's story, we see her lack of self-worth was based on her perceived failings as a parent. That resulted in additional angst related to what she could do to give her children a sense of normalcy and a happy home.

Women like Laura often compromise their own dreams and aspirations in order to ensure their children are happy. Divorced or single parents often give *even more* of themselves up to make up for the perceived gap in their child's life. Others in bad relationships will stay stuck because they're afraid to upset the status quo. They stay in dysfunctional relationships to protect their kids.

In Laura's case, she'd decided to keep her second husband's name so that her daughter would have the same name as her. Over time, Laura realized there was a cost in keeping a name that didn't fit her. Holding onto that name didn't serve her or her daughter. In the end, Laura decided to take back her family name. It was an important step on the journey to embracing her authentic self.

Let's put this all in perspective: Laura had low self-worth as a mother. She believed her own inability to love her children "well enough" compromised their development and that she wasn't deserving of their love due to her own perceived failings as a mother.

Then, through open and vulnerable communication with her kids, she reached a breakthrough in her relationship with her kids. Laura's vulnerability, which was rooted in authenticity, brought a degree of forgiveness when Laura let go of the guilt. This launched her towards a truer understanding of herself as someone who wanted to live a life of service by helping children.

Next, she examined her excitement about Italy and realized that it was based on ego rather than a deep connection. Putting those pieces together allowed Laura to realize that, in her core, she sought an existence free of the need to appear a certain way in others' eyes. Laura wanted contentment, happiness and to feel connected and fulfilled.

Finally, Laura looked at the name she'd carried for several years and recognized that it wasn't an authentic representation of herself. With a new understanding of why authenticity mattered, Laura realized that her quest for authenticity would gain momentum if she went back to using her family name.

Laura's story demonstrates why I encourage people to look at their lives from within. A close examination of our stories helps us uncover—and comprehend—the inner turmoil. It also enables us to understand why small external changes promote such massive internal change.

WHICH CHANGE HOLDS THE KEY?

I was running a weekend seminar not long ago when a gentleman showed up on crutches. He explained that he'd sprained his ankle that weekend.

As we progressed through the weekend, this gentleman opened

up and discussed what he felt was his greatest challenge. As he listed the details of that challenge, I stopped him mid-sentence. I then asked, with no small amount of genuine curiosity, about a completely different aspect of his life.

With a confused and rather frustrated look in his eye he told me, "I don't see the point; in fact I see no relevance between that and the challenge I want to focus on." At this stage of the day, the man was sitting at a table with his injured leg propped up on a chair. He was periodically icing the injured leg with ice and towels supplied by the hotel where the event was being held.

I then looked at him and asked what happened to his leg. He said he sprained his ankle hiking in the mountains of British Columbia. He then went on to explain that he went to the doctor and the doctor had recommended that the ankle remain bandaged, that he keep the weight off it using crutches to walk and that he ice the ankle to minimize swelling.

Because my question about his leg failed to diffuse his frustration about the first question I'd asked, he said again, "I still don't get why you want me to talk about this particular area when I outlined very clearly what my greatest challenge is."

I replied, "When you went to the doctor and he told you to bandage, elevate, and ice your ankle, did you say 'No. I'm not going to do one of those things because in isolation it will not fix the issue?' No. What you did was trust that doing all three would result in a positive outcome for full recovery."

I can't tell you how many times someone has sat in front of me and insisted their challenge lies solely in one area. When I ask them if they think another area has anything to do with the situation, they typically reject the notion that another aspect of life could influence the area they want to talk about.

Facing problems that appear unrelated to a focus issue is often the best way to shine a light on the challenges we've already identified. Life can be complicated. That's why a series of small revelations can create the lasting and sustainable change that tackling a major challenge cannot.

Indeed, small tweaks create big changes, and proof of this is found in Guinness. Let me explain. A few years back, I brought a group of clients on a tour of the Guinness factory in Ireland. The Managing Director came and spoke to us and I was fascinated when he explained that a three-degree change to the serving temperature of Guinness alters the taste by 50%.

That's right. It's the small tweaks that make big changes.

THE INNER GAME

Many approaches to personal growth focus on the external changes we make in order to grow. They assume that if we undertake a better routine from the morning until night, we will be more productive.

They believe that if we start our day with positive mantras, we'll be in the right state of mind to make positive change. These approaches argue that daily exercise gives people the strength and courage to make life changes. Proponents even advocate that people hang out with a higher quality of friend.

There's some merit to these ideas. But when all is said and done, they are external approaches to personal growth. They depend on external changes without recognizing that this can only affect external circumstances. The end results are, by necessity, temporary. Why? Because the momentum for authentic change must be generated internally.

My philosophy is based on the notion that the answers to our challenges are within. If we want to make real, lasting change in our fitness, we first have to believe we deserve the body we say we want. By the same token, if we want to create a better routine for our workday, we must first know that we're working on the right thing. If we want to speak positive mantras, we have to believe what we're saying.

The bottom line is that real change depends on intense, and sometimes painful, self-reflection. It's difficult to convey in writing how much work this process was for Laura. But powerful realizations don't drop out of the sky; they're the result of a kind of work that very few people do: self-work.

There are many approaches one can take to access this inner path towards authentic change. Sadly, the door to the soul often remains closed until forced open by a difficult experience.

Many people arrive on my doorstep when they feel a little lost or unclear about the future. Others come because they want to ensure that they are on the right path towards a life of real meaning.

Then there are the people who have hit a wall through a dramatic life event that has pushed them into a corner, making them ready for change.

These life events run the gamut of human experience. Some are reeling from the loss of a spouse. Others are confronting family, health or business struggles that forced them to re-examine priorities.

While the incentive to make positive life changes sometimes result from negative circumstances, no one needs to wait for problems before they take back control of their lives. We're all able to access our inner wisdom and make real change from the inside. It requires self-work, but I urge you to be the person who pursues positive change versus being the individual upon whom change is thrust.

My strategy with this chapter was to illustrate how an unauthentic self-identity exacts a negative toll on our lives. I hope you are empowered by the idea that small shifts towards a more authentic self-identity can improve our relationship to ourselves, thereby transforming our relationships with every other aspect of our lives!

CHAPTER 7:

THE STARVING ARTIST

"The brave always win."
~ Philip McKernan

FINDING ONE'S SOUL THROUGH PASSION

A lot of us have experienced what it's like to take the wrong turn on a path. Getting back on track is typically a matter of figuring out where we went wrong and steering back on course. A lot of us also know people who die with regrets. These people got off course—and couldn't find their way back. Sadly, this phenomenon is as common as it is avoidable!

Several of the work/life experiences for which I'm most grateful include the special opportunities I get to work alongside people transitioning from one career to another. Dean was one such man, but did not know it when we met.

Dean began playing music as a young child. Growing up, music always had a place in his life. But while music was his first love and his passion, the practical-minded young man decided to study business when he entered university. Even though he seriously considered pursuing studies in music, Dean put intellect over heart. He was, in his own words, determined not "to be a starving artist."

After completing an undergraduate degree in business, Dean continued his business education with an MBA. He was a highly intelligent and driven individual and did well all through his studies, and into the early years of his career.

Dean first worked as an accountant as this was his specialty coming out of university. While he was good at his job, Dean knew he had bigger ambitions. In search of the "next big challenge," Dean found himself in a real estate guru's seminar. Young, skilled and smart, Dean rightfully had a great deal of external confidence in his abilities. He was also somewhat naïve, a state-of-mind that left him susceptible to messages of untold success. Caught up in the story of the real estate dream, Dean imagined he could make millions—and one day get back to the music he loved.

Sitting in a room with hundreds of others simultaneously envisioning how they would transform themselves from ordinary wage earners to lives built on passive income, Dean bought into the dream of using real estate wealth to create a dream future.

Dean went on a mission to build a massive and profitable real estate portfolio. Following a remarkable series of steps, he began raising money for residential real estate investments from within his circle of contacts. Dean's enthusiasm and knowledge of booming markets in Western Canada, coupled with his intelligence, made for a compelling sales pitch. Most of the money Dean raised came from his own family and friends. Dean's own parents were investors, too. They trustingly dipped into their life's savings to buy houses with Dean and the business partner Dean picked up early in his move into real estate. With his business partner's help, Dean convinced several money partners to invest in their business.

Investing with family and friends is a much trickier business than most people assume. Dean's parents believed in the economic potential of the investments they were making. But their special connection to Dean meant they were emotionally connected to the outcome, too.

Over a relatively short period of time, Dean and his partner acquired 75 rental properties without investing any of their own money. All the required cash came from silent money partners. In the early days, the investments went along as planned. The duo built their portfolio and with investment gurus still bullish on the market's long-term potential, Dean and his partner expected that market appreciation would soon make them wealthy.

Unfortunately for Dean and his investors, reality was not as rosy as the gurus suggested. Their business projections required strong rents. When vacancy in the resource-based town they'd invested in shot up, their portfolio started to cost them money. One month, Dean reported cash flow in the thousands. Months later, it was thousands of dollars to the negative. With lenders still requiring mortgages be paid, the sudden market shift spelled big trouble for Dean and his partner.

To make matters worse, the value of the properties dropped, and there were no buyers, either. With selling not an option, Dean was stuck in a horrible financial situation. The only options he had were bad options. The company was in emergency mode.

Before long, Dean was forced to sign some units over to investors. Other units went into foreclosure. It was messy, and to this day, several years later, Dean is still extricating himself from the tax and accounting aspects of the business.

It's no surprise that Dean was demoralized by the events. A business model built on a "dream future" had collapsed. Worse yet, Dean knew his parents had invested much of their savings in his failed business. He knew they wouldn't be getting their money back soon, if ever.

In addition to their financial loss, Dean's parents were stuck with the additional burden of trying to manage the properties Dean had signed over to them. With the market dead and the properties more than 1,000 km from their home, this was not an easy task. Shifty property managers and a transient population conspired to make their lives as property investors a struggle.

SOLACE IN PASSION

In the midst of his personal and financial struggles, Dean courageously went back to his music, albeit with some persuasion. I can't begin to express how much courage this decision took. Conventional thinking states that Dean should never have taken up his music at the moment his business was folding. I say screw conventional thinking—and Dean did, too.

You see, through all of this, Dean harboured a dream to make income from his music. He was still adverse to the notion of being a "starving artist," but he knew he needed to pursue his passion.

After all, that decision to study business instead of music had contributed to Dean's experience with unmitigated financial disaster by encouraging him to choose profits over passion.

Stepping back from Dean's story for a minute, I want you to think about the strange choice we make when we chase money.

When we truly love something and its practice makes us feel full and complete, we are fulfilled and happy. When we turn it off to chase money we have to pretend we're something we're not. Any value we get from that pursuit is, by definition, based on false self-worth.

This is exactly what Dean did, and result speaks for itself. Perhaps it was the drastic nature of Dean's situation that made him turn back to his music. I'm not certain how he got the courage, but making music a life priority was essential to Dean's journey back to himself.

In the early days, Dean's commitment to his music was almost a retreat. But it brought him comfort, so he stuck with it. First he played, and then he started teaching, initially at no charge. At that point, it wasn't about making money, nor should it have been. Passion is *self*-validating in that it doesn't require income to be validated. I'm always amused when people say they won't pursue their passion because they can't monetize it. Think about it: is it really a passion if monetization is a condition of its expression or pursuit?

Every time I saw him after he started playing again, Dean looked more relaxed and happy. As he stepped into his music, he started stripping away his misconceptions about what he could or could not accomplish along the way.

Lo and behold, Dean's business experience, education, and acumen suddenly had a proper purpose. Instead of putting himself in that place where many artists struggle, Dean started thinking of novel ways to make money from his music. That wasn't a condition of his playing, it was a bonus!

Because Dean understood business, he was able to envision a

life where music could provide an income. More importantly, because he now understood himself, Dean began to believe he deserved the personal fulfillment that came with following his passion. While Dean was still very occupied with unwinding his real estate business, he started to see a future of passion and profit.

The fact that Dean was finding himself again was no small feat considering what he'd been through over the previous years of disconnected business pursuits.

Dean also agreed a way to pay back some of the money he had borrowed from his parents in time. His parents also took some responsibility for their own actions on this front.

WEARING THE HANNIBAL MASK

If you've never seen the movie, *Silence of the Lambs*, let me explain the significance of masks in that story. In sum, Hannibal Lecter, the evil dude of the movie, famously wears two separate masks.

The first mask is worn when he's transported into his prison cell. It restrains him from being able to bite any of the guards as they try to transport him. After he manages to attack and kill one of the guards, Hannibal actually cuts off the guard's face and puts the skin over his own face. This second mask of human flesh allows Hannibal to trick the other guards into carrying him out of the cell. It enables his escape.

When we say someone is "wearing a mask," we typically mean they're pretending (often unaware) to be something they're not. As a result, they end up being someone they're not happy with.

Dean wasn't just wearing a mask; he was wearing an entire costume along with a Hannibal Lecter mask made of steel and chained up with padlocks. I exaggerate for effect. But the truth is that Dean's heart and soul longed to play music. At his very core, Dean wanted to be himself—a fully self-expressed individual playing music and living life on his terms.

However, Dean was seduced by the business success he projected when he put on his pinstripe suit. That suit projected a message of being in full control. It also projected a message of success, at least by standard definition.

What Dean did in building a large real estate portfolio in a short period of time is not common. Of the hundreds of people sitting in the guru's room with Dean that day, it wouldn't be implausible to suggest that only a handful purchased properties at a similar rate as Dean.

This says nothing about the authenticity of the other hundreds of people in the room. It's likely that most of them were as caught up as Dean was in the dream of real estate success. Dean just happened to be more efficient at getting himself in deep real estate trouble.

What happened next is interesting. When Dean realized that he was a leader in the real estate community—and that others wanted to be like him—he basked in the admiration of his colleagues. It's little wonder that he also started to want to be like the gurus in the room. Dean wanted the "success" these people talk about. But he also wanted to be the guy talking.

The end result was that this venture (which became a kind of adventure) took Dean further and further from himself. When that ended, he found himself stripped of his source of false confidence. Having the mask ripped off forced Dean to rediscover his true essence. He needed to learn (again) what it means to be truly confident versus pseudo confident.

EXAMINING DEAN'S *WHY*

Dean's story seems like a simple version of the age-old story about how people who chase lofty financial goals get lost along the way. If you look closer, a more important truth appears. And the crux of that truth is that Dean wasn't only driven by money.

He was also driven by what he thought money would provide.

In sum, the wealth gurus Dean was listening to painted a picture of an unlimited *future* where those with wealth can pursue their passions with unlimited free time and plenty of money.

In Dean's case, he believed pursuing music would lead him into the life of an impoverished artist. Determined to avoid that, Dean chose to pursue an avenue that did not assume poverty. When the wealth guru sold him a package that included putting his passion aside to make big money, what Dean really heard was that he would eventually be able to pursue his passion. Whereas accounting left no room for passion, real estate virtually promised it. That's right. The false belief that pushed him off track maintained that Dean had to put his music aside to be able to come back to music later.

I'm not belittling Dean's choices. But I do want to emphasize the bizarre reality of his choices. Dean didn't just rob himself of something he actually loved, he replaced it with prison. Dean's story illustrates my aversion for the term, "financial freedom." This pursuit of money for a better tomorrow is, in a nutshell, the reason so many wealthy people never attain the ultimate freedom: peace of mind.

Let me explain this disconnect another way, again using Mother Teresa as an example. What if this renowned humanitarian stood in front of a sick person while holding the medicine that person needed to be well, then turned away from that individual without administering the medication. Some people who want to change the world may follow a passion that encourages them to build an empire first. But that wasn't Mother Teresa's way. She believed today was an important as tomorrow—and that passion guided her actions.

Unfortunately, millions of people make short-sighted life choices every day, often because they're so focused on the future they don't acknowledge today. Some people, for example, will literally do anything to pay the mortgage, but not take the simplest actions to honor their souls, passions, and health. Putting off happiness and joy in the present for an imagined future, that may or may not ever come, is a widespread problem.

I commend Dean for the changes he made. It wasn't easy, and he showed enormous bravery. Part of Dean's why was informed by a desire to get back to music. This desire, coupled with his aversion to the image of the starving artist, made it easy for him to follow promises of future riches. It also made it easy for him to think he had to give up music while on the path to wealth. That was his own choice, and he made it with dollar signs in his eyes.

It's important to note that Dean's pursuit of future wealth fed a greater self-belief that he wasn't good enough just as he was. It wasn't an authentic self-belief. The dogged pursuit of a particular dream is one way that many of us are encouraged to don false masks. In reality, Dean's self-belief going into that guru's seminar was so low he felt more comfortable in the Hannibal masks than in his own skin.

This lack of self-belief wasn't visible to most of the people who were watching Dean from the outside. When wearing his real estate investor costume, Dean derived an empowering sense of confidence. He felt special. He felt important. People came to listen to him talk, gave him their money and asked his opinion about real estate markets and the economy. Like everyone in the room, Dean just wanted acceptance—and he was getting that, and more.

While his initial motivation might have been to build a business that could support the life he *really* wanted to live, it didn't take Dean long to slip into *being* someone else. His why was now based on external drivers, and once that happened, he was no longer in control of his life.

He was an actor playing a role in a movie script he didn't write and wasn't directing. Dean might have thought his movie would end well, but he didn't recognize the parallels to the storyline of *Titanic*. That's too bad. Because Dean stepped onto a sinking ship the moment he started faking that his passion was tied to having a lot of money.

The fact that there's a cost to every action we take should come as no surprise to any adult reading this book. As adults, we should feel compelled to calculate if the cost of our actions are worth it. For Dean, the cost was grave. He gave up music, built his own prison, and was known to others only by his masks. The cost to Dean was a loss of self. After his investment woes, nothing less than a total rebuild of his life would be good enough for Dean. Fortunately for him, that's what Dean did when the movie stopped. Given his abiding fear of the starving artist, however, this transition was far from easy.

And how could it be? Dean's fear of the starving artist was formed in his early years. He carried that false belief with him for a very long time, allowing it to influence his academic studies and to risk "losing it all" when he decided music was something he could enjoy only after he accumulated much wealth. By the time Dean's real estate dream left him broke, ashamed and disillusioned, the little bit of time he gave to even thinking about music was the only authentic pinprick of light in his massively inauthentic (and fundamentally dark) existence. Do you see how incredible this is? In his heart, Dean always thought of himself as an artist. He had a false belief that artists were poor, so he ended up poor even though he wasn't practicing his art. It's sad to know that a belief formed in Dean's youth, however misinformed, could cause him to act in such unhealthy and unfulfilling ways.

When Dean started digging to the bottom of his false beliefs, and looking within for real answers, he found happiness, peace of mind and financial success. Better still, he found it in the very thing he loved, his music.

KNOWING ONE'S SELF

You might think I'm saying everyone who is not currently monetizing their passion must throw off the chains of their current work situation and jump into their passion with both feet.

This is not true. I don't believe that. There's often space for continuing in a current job or business— perhaps indefinitely.

However, I believe everyone should search within for their passion and lean into it. This leaning in, should not be conditional on making money from it. Ironically, it's the leaning in itself that yields the opportunities to earn income from one's passion. Doing this is about knowing one's self. It's about understanding what drives you at the core. What would the world have lost if Mother Teresa, whose good work continued even after she died, focused on monetizing her passion instead of just doing it?

Or what about Nelson Mandela? He didn't live a life of glamor and excess. He worked as a lawyer before going to prison, but his focus was on representing clients in a system that denied them legal assistance and on improving the conditions of his fellow South Africans. Ultimately, his goal was to end apartheid and live in a completely free and just society. This was his passion. And one cannot even say that following that passion brought pleasure to Mandela's life. I think it's fair to say that Nelson Mandela's passion brought meaning to his life, but slapped him in the face every day.

First-world men like Dean are typically sheltered from harsh circumstances. Dean's passion for the more prosaic pursuit of music obviously lacks the urgency of a Mandela-level pursuit. But that doesn't negate its value to Dean's life. Instead of developing a sophisticated plan to first monetize, then live, Mandela just *lived* his truth. It's so simple yet so powerful. The true power in Dean's life began to materialize when he became clear about what he *really* wanted. Once he'd stripped away the false belief about the starving artist, he freed himself to create, and that's the very thing for which his soul longed. Once Dean started living his life as an artist, the path materialized.

During my group mentoring sessions and retreats, I often have people stand before me and articulate reasons why they can't do something. My response, often delivered with some thought provoking sarcasm, is always the same: "I know you can't do it, but what would you do if you could do it?" The answers I get after that are invariably simple—and stunning.

For example, once Dean was able to quiet down the internal voice that told him all artists are poor, he went to work creating a beautiful life. Financial success as an artist followed.

To do that, Dean had to *allow* himself to go after his music. Why would someone riddled with guilt and shame about a failed investment business feel he *deserves* to make money from the thing he loves? It was a struggle to even allow himself to think about music never mind give himself permission to think about how he might make money from it. It would be unfair to suggest that Dean's transformation was sparked by changing a single belief. Before he could create the kind of internal space where a new dream could develop, Dean had to acknowledge his shame and start to forgive himself. Once he started doing that, hope was possible and he began to practice music because it brought him pleasure. The simple act of doing something he'd loved since childhood then gave him the space where he could begin to believe he deserved to be happy.

And Dean's success wasn't about hugging trees and pursuing happiness at all costs. As a smart guy with solid business experience—good and bad—it didn't take long before Dean saw an opportunity to monetize his passion by setting up an educational component to his business. In the first week he launched his online music academy he made $25,000 for five days work.

My main point here is that the truth will set you free, and following a false truth will make you a prisoner of your own life. Worse yet, you'll be condemned to living a life behind someone else's mask!

CHAPTER 8:

THE ANGRY "SPIRITUAL" WOMAN

"Success is manufactured in the mind
while happiness is cultivated in the soul."
~ Philip McKernan

BELIEF BASED SELF-SABOTAGE

Have you ever been shocked to learn about a belief you hold? We tend to think that we know ourselves better than anyone else, yet many hold to a belief system that's little more than a mask. In truth, we all have blind spots when it comes to knowing who we really are, and these blind spots can be crippling.

As you saw with Dean's story, passion can provide solace in the moment and a way back to our authentic path. In this chapter, you'll learn how our own blind spots lead us to self-sabotage the journey to our authentic path, and therefore a life of meaning.

THE SPIRITUAL LADY

Diane is a wonderful lady with a life story full of incredible beauty and heartbreaking pain. A full-time artist who creates beautiful paintings, Diane channels her personal feelings into beautiful art.

When I met Diane at a business-marketing program, she was struggling with her own version of the starving artist paradigm and seeking ways to make herself financially viable as an artist. There were several hundred people at this event, and the focus was how to improve marketing efforts.

At the time, Diane was taking several courses about marketing. She was learning how to use Twitter, Facebook, and blogging to market herself as an artist so that she could be profitable doing the thing she loved.

Diane creates remarkable paintings and her daily routine is focused on creation. She pours her heart onto the canvas every day, with each painting creating an expression of her soul.

While her work fed the creative side of who Diane is, she struggled to make ends meet. Her inability to make a living as an artist fuelled self-doubt about her work—and whether she was "good enough" to make it.

As we got to know each other better, Diane told me about a doctor she knew. According to Diane, this doctor was completely driven by money. Although Diane considered him a friend, she was candid about her disrespect for his money-obsessed approach to life.

I was intrigued to see her disrespect expressed as *anger*. She was angry about the doctor's money obsession and the mere mention of it evoked a strong response in Diane. Seeing this vitriol from an otherwise calm and peaceful person who actually defined herself as someone "spiritual." I challenged her about money. It may not have been clear to her, but it was obvious to me.

I even told her I thought she hated money. I said, "You think you're bad at marketing and that you're a bad businessperson, but is it possible that you just hate money." Her response was, "Philip, I know you're good, but I think you're way off on this one."

Once again I ventured into the lion's den as I could sense her anger under her beautiful mask. I asked her if she felt like she had anger within her. While she assured me that was not the case, but admitted that my questioning was pissing her off.

We both got a glimpse of the anger she was carrying within her. She remained, however, mostly blind to the reality that she was an intelligent, beautiful and creative person—who was also very angry.

When it comes to anger, we think of people throwing chairs across the room or physically fighting as an expression of the anger. The reality is everyone has anger, and it's often the ones who are not in touch with it, that are the most angry.

We hear a lot about fear and the need to overcome, dominate or eradicate it. I would take fear any day over blind anger. Anger is a destructive force that blocks us from loving ourselves and allowing ourselves to be loved.

Certain I *was not* off the mark, I further pressed her about her beliefs around money. I said, "Here you are, spending every day deep in creation and making beautiful works of art. Then you must take the very thing you love and ask others to give you money—the very thing you hate—for something you love. That must be excruciating."

Diane grabbed her stomach, and crumpled over, much like someone who'd been punched in the belly. I've never in my life seen someone have such an intense physical response to learning the truth of their belief system. She sobbed uncontrollably for several minutes before finally composing herself enough to confront her own truth. "I hate money," said Diane.

STIFLING CREATIVITY

Diane's external problem was that she wasn't making enough money as an artist. From that outside-looking-in perspective, she had two choices. She could embrace her role as a starving artist or develop better marketing strategies to improve sales. Few would recognize the real problem: Diane was sabotaging herself. Because she hated money, she didn't want to earn it!

While marketing strategies might help some people, the tool itself doesn't provide the kind of answers people like Diane need. There are millions of ways to succeed in any business, even if the business involves making, selling and teaching art. But a strategy in and of itself, no matter how "right" it is for the particular business, doesn't guarantee success.

That's because strategies or a lack thereof, are not the problem! What's more important is what we believe about ourselves and how that impacts our success and happiness. Dean's belief system equated artistry with poverty. This was a problem for him because he wanted to be wealthy. To stay true to his belief that money was the worthy pursuit, Dean decided he couldn't pursue his music until later. Although his path was misguided, Dean saw music as a kind of reward for financial success. It was something he could do "later."

Diane laboured under a different delusion. She believed that money was bad. And this wasn't a casual distrust. Diane *hated* money. Hating money might not have been so destructive to her business if she was selling widgets or plastic gadgets. But since Diane was selling her *art*, creations with an obvious connection to her soul, Diane felt like every sale was a choice between something she loved, and something she hated.

Diane's situation was complicated by the fact that she talks about her art coming from an almost divine source. Believing that her work is inspired, she holds a deep connection to every piece of art she creates. There's no way she could be happy about trading her work for any amount of money. Given this money mindset, is it any wonder she had a hard time attracting enough money into her life to be financially viable as an artist?

And that's the dilemma! Since Diane chose the path of a professional artist, she needed to sell her work. To do that, she needed to understand that the art she created was not solely for her. It was meant to be enjoyed by other people, some of whom would pay her for the privilege of owning her work.

Intellectually, Diane could accept this work-for-sale dynamic. Unfortunately, however, her hatred of money tainted the process of creation. Knowing she now painted for money, she struggled to paint at all! Is it any wonder Diane believed money was behind the destruction of all she loved?

As we've seen throughout this book, our beliefs, even those falsely held, have enormous power. Once we're *aware* of those beliefs, we can do something about them. But as long as we live our lives unaware of our true belief systems, we are stuck believing that we're *broken*. Diane was in her forties and unaware of this deeply held belief, until now.

Diane was one of those people who thinks she's broken. In fact, nothing could be further from the truth. She was and is a stunning individual with a brilliant present and a brilliant future. She just happened to have what so many people have, a belief that didn't serve her.

It's not as though my conversation with Diane solved all her problems. Growth is always a process, but I can report that with improved understanding of what was really holding her business back, Diane has been better able to monetize her art. By releasing some of the pressure she felt around money's dark side, she positioned herself to push past the starving artist mould. Now selling more art and teaching others, she creates every day—and is happier for it.

THE RIPPLE EFFECT

But helping Diane acknowledge her hatred for money did more than enhance her business life. In truth, these feelings caused a negative ripple effect in all of her relationships. Diane obviously knew people who earned money and enjoyed what it did for their lives. These individuals were objects of derision for Diane—even when she actually *wanted* to like them. Of course this caused her a lot of sadness as people disappeared from her life, especially since Diane also continued to self-sabotage her attempts to succeed financially as an artist.

Since she was previously unaware of her belief, Diane's efforts to "fix" her financial situation were for naught. Her story reminds me of a man who participated in one of my recent mentoring programs. The simple question began with me asking the group of business owners, "what is the biggest business challenge you have right now?"

This man was adamant that his number one challenge was to seek out the right cash flowing solutions for his business, a chain of restaurants. Determined to expand this business, he had put aside everything in his life for several months. He assured me, and others in the room, that this all-or-nothing approach was essential to his business growth strategy. As I've heard that story more than a few times, I prodded him to tell us more. I didn't buy his answer and after some dialogue I asked him the same question again. He let out a sigh and said, "I'm not sure I'm in the right business."

I wasn't even surprised. I've seen turnarounds like his enough times to know that people who appear driven in a particular direction often learn they're not on the right path. But once you've got momentum, it can be hard to turn a train around! As you can imagine, the conversation changed dramatically when he made that admission.

Diane's story is no different. Although her truth was buried much deeper and it took a lot more excavating, she and this other businessman both arrived at the same realization: although they hadn't known it, they were self-sabotaging their own precious work to add meaning to their lives. I urge you to excavate your own belief system and find out what you believe. Facing the truth is the most powerful action you can take.

That's especially true when you learn to face your inner truth and then share it with others. That step demands *vulnerability*, the fundamental value of which is the subject of my next chapter.

THE 4 TYPES OF BELIEFS

How could a women walk this earth for forty years and not be in touch with the deeply held belief that she, at some level, was broken? In essence she believed she was not good enough.

To understand beliefs, I believe we need to separate the different types of beliefs in order to explore their authenticity.

1. ADOPTED BELIEFS

These are the beliefs that we take on from others. The most common source of these types of beliefs come from our parents. Religion is one such belief that we don't often question. Indeed, it's often assumed that the spiritual path our parents are on is one we share with them. It's important that we question these beliefs in order to embrace them as our own, or make course corrections towards our own authentic beliefs.

We are often too concerned with upsetting our parents to even questions these beliefs for ourselves, never mind do anything about them.

2. LIMITING BELIEFS

These are the ones that are more commonly talked about when it comes to personal growth, and they are relativity easy to uncover. An example of a limiting belief when it comes to money would be, "money is evil."

These beliefs hold us back and often create conscious self-sabotage.

3. DEBILITATING BELIEFS

I refer to these beliefs as the stealth bombers. They elude our consciousness but play out none-the-less. They are the ones we are unaware of which makes them even more dangerous.

On a recent call with a client, I inquired about the quality of her relationship with her two children. She assured me she had a "great relationship" with them, and in fact wanted to move the conversation along.

"How do you know," I asked. She went on to explain the type of interaction they have and opened up a little more. As the conversation unfolded, I learned the truth was that these relationships were in fact good, but not great. Now we can get to work on that.

4. OUR TRUE BELIEFS

These are the truths we truly stand for; the ones that come from our being that we cannot be talked or bought out of. The issue with our true beliefs is that we sometimes get them mixed up with the others. This leads us to tell ourselves that we believe something when in actual fact, we don't.

The lady I mentioned above knew deep down her relationship with her kids was somewhat flat. The pain of admitting it kept her from the truth, and that in turn, kept her from recognizing opportunities to change it.

CHAPTER 9:

TURNING SHAME TO INSPIRATION

"You can leave the playground bully behind,
but you can't run from the bully in the mirror."
~ Philip McKernan

SPEAKING OUR TRUTH

Any discovery of truth, especially in our inner relationship with ourselves, leads to powerful realizations about what's holding us back from fulfillment—and what it will take to move us forward. However, to be truly transformative, truth must come from a place of vulnerability. While I've been using this concept in my practice for many years, it's becoming more commonly accepted. And I believe that's a very good thing, since truth and vulnerability are, in my experience, a powerful combination.

Have you ever shared a deeply held emotion with another person or a group of people? How was that experience?

Whether it happens on purpose or accidentally, these kinds of revelations are part of what I call the practice of vulnerability. When we're vulnerable with others we can never predict how they will respond. Sometimes people react negatively to vulnerability. Other times, they might be uncomfortable. This usually says more about the listener than about the speaker.

However, in other circumstances, when the listener is ready for the message and responds with compassion and vulnerability in return, the result is a stunning coming together of human beings sharing compassion.

In the previous chapter, we discussed how excavating our belief system can be enormously powerful. Here, we'll see how taking our truth a step further, by sharing it vulnerably with others, can create incredible good will and transformation.

THE BULLY WITHIN

A mentoring client named Carrie called me one day and asked for some advice about an upcoming talk she planned to give before a public-speaking group to which she belonged. It was her first public presentation to the group. Being a perfectionist, she was determined to do a great job and she came to me for some insight into her chosen topic. Carrie had joined this small group because she wanted to do more public speaking. When she asked for my advice, I countered with questions about what she had planned. Carrie launched into a detailed description of her topic, which would be about goal-setting.

Being a good Irishman, I admit that I often use sarcasm as a tool to challenge the people I coach and mentor. I don't use it to be rude. I use it to help them surpass hurdles they've often erected in their own paths. So, when Carrie told me about her topic, I responded, "Oh wow Carrie, I'm so inspired that you're going to give a talk on goal-setting."

The phone went quiet—but I could hear her seething rage. Known for her own fieriness, Carrie's anger did not surprise me.

After the silent (yet strangely angry) pause, she started to speak. And I could tell she wasn't impressed with me. After all, she'd taken some time and care to craft her presentation. I knew that. I also knew that what she really wanted was for me to tell her what she wanted to hear. Her silence betrayed the fact that she was looking for something along the lines of: "Wow. You nailed it, what a great message. You will blow them away."

I wanted her to see the value in expecting more. "All kidding aside," said I, "what is one thing you would be scared to speak about because you might not be able to hold back tears?" Her response was immediate and unflinching, "bullying."

And this is where she got my "wow." I said, "Wow, you didn't even second guess yourself for a moment. I didn't know you were bullied as a kid." Again there was silence on the other end, but this time it wasn't anger.

When Carrie spoke again she said, "No Philip, I was the bully." Now I was intrigued. "Why don't you speak about bullying?" I asked.

"Because, Philip, I might cry," she replied.

"Well, speak about it and cry," I said.

Carrie went on to tell me about her life in junior high and high school. She explained how girls bully, how it's different from boys, and how she picked on certain girls.

She also told me about the outcome of the bullying. She told me about how horrified she was years later when she realized the pain she caused others. I knew this was the talk she had to give. If Carrie was serious about honing her oral presentation skills, she had to get serious about what she was willing to talk about. As she told me about her earlier experiences, Carrie moved the goal-setting talk to the back burner and resolved to talk about bullying instead.

After some more thought and using *much* courage, Carrie gave the bully talk. The decision made her vulnerable—and real. She cried, they cried, and she received a standing ovation. It was her first-ever oral presentation—and Carrie rocked!

She wasn't expecting this result. Like many, Carrie didn't have the highest self-belief. She even expected to be ridiculed by her audience, or worse, rejected. Instead she received a standing ovation that included long-time club members who'd heard hundreds of first-time speeches.

When I next spoke to her, Carrie was thrilled with the result. Interestingly enough, she's also decided she wouldn't pursue more talks until she got her own house in order. I was stunned and knew I had to push her to go outside her comfort zone. I said, "Oh, excuse me; I thought I was speaking with someone who actually cared about people. You obviously don't, it's all about you." Sarcasm again.

I went on to explain I felt she was using her past experiences, including some shame related to those experiences, to avoid having to share her message with the world even though it could have a very positive impact. This is a pattern common to perfectionists.

Because she didn't want to start a process that would make her vulnerable, Carrie was trying to step back into her comfort zone. As Carrie and I had a good relationship, she couldn't dismiss my comment—and its challenge. Instead, she used my comment as rocket fuel. Within a couple of weeks, Carrie was giving her bully talk at a local school. In one month, she spoke five more times—a courageous move that brought her message to hundreds of kids in different schools.

GIVING PEOPLE WHAT YOU THINK THEY WANT

The experience was empowering. Some school kids broke down as she spoke. Others came up to her after the talk and shared their own stories. The most important audience of all, the kids themselves, thus affirmed that Carrie did the right talk. And the hidden gift was for Carrie. Even though she knew she wanted to speak to groups and make an inspiring impact on other people's lives, she did not know how she would be able to do so.

By speaking from the heart, Carrie's bullying talk helped her realize how "easy" it can be to inspire people when you speak from a place of truth. But what Carrie did wasn't easy. It was simple, but it wasn't easy. It was simple because it was uncomplicated in that Carrie told her own story. But sharing that story was far from easy because it forced Carrie to come to face a part of her life that brought her—and others—much pain. To accomplish this powerful feat, Carrie really had to access her soul.

When I posed the simple question, "what's one thing you'd have a hard time speaking about because you'd have trouble holding back tears?" she knew immediately. It's so simple. The world would be better if we shared the messages that were simple, but not easy.

When people tell me they don't know what they want from a particular situation, or from life itself, I never believe them. Experience has shown me that people *always* know. Helping people get out of their own way forms a large portion of the work I do. In this case, Carrie knew goal setting wasn't the message she needed to speak about. Isn't it interesting to think she was ready to get up in front of a large group and pretend it was the "best" she could do.

Carrie's strategy is not uncommon. People are often preoccupied with giving people what we think they want rather than giving them what's in our heart. This preoccupation leads to anxiety. It's like we're "scared into" doing something—even though we know it's not what we need to do. We are so desperate for acceptance that we'd rather tell people what they think we want to hear than to be honest with them about what we need to say.

A lot of people go through life focused on finding out what people want and then finding ways to deliver it. The great fallacy of that approach is that people don't always know what they want from us. To be honest, we often love it when people give us something we didn't expect, or more than we expect. That's what made Carrie's first bully talk so wonderful. She believed her audience wanted to be inspired. When she tapped into the message at her core, she gave them something they weren't expecting, and the result was stunning.

> *"People don't know what they want until you give it to them."*
> ~ *Steve Jobs*

Carrie's bully talks proved Steve Jobs was correct. How was anyone supposed to know what he or she wanted from Carrie? She hadn't told anyone about her bullying past. Until challenged to talk about something that really mattered to her, she didn't even know that bullying remained such a major issue in her life.

Now take a step back from Carrie's story and acknowledge that there's a voice inside each of us that's trying to tell us what really matters. It comes from our core and it tells us how we could inspire the people around us. Developing this voice, and letting it evolve from a whisper to a thunderclap, is a powerful way to unleash our enormous potential on the world.

But how can we do this? To find our voices, our authentic voices, we need to understand that what's inside is exactly what we need to give the world. By trying to deliver what we think others want, we often limit the opportunity to make an impact. Carrie's example is living proof.

VULNERABILITY WILL SET YOU FREE

Most of us are terrified to be vulnerable. We believe vulnerability is a sign of weakness. The thought of crying publicly is enough to make us want to curl up in the foetal position.

When I asked Carrie why she wouldn't give the bullying talk, her immediate response was she didn't want to cry in front of her audience. She was scared to death of vulnerability. She was scared to death of being judged. She was terrified of rejection, of not being loved.

So why is it that we don't want people to really see us? Why is vulnerability so difficult even though it can be the one experience that sets us free? I believe that a willingness to be vulnerable sets the stage for us to break down barriers between us and others. It does this by creating the kind of trust that brings people together.

What it really does is inspire others to be vulnerable in return. Vulnerability is the bridge that connects one authentic human being to another.

This is what gives vulnerability its power. Most human interaction involves a shallow playing out of pre-determined roles (acting). True vulnerability is rare, touching, and fundamentally humanizing.

During my events, I've had several people say to me something along these lines, "When I'm in this room, I know exactly what I want to do and what I need to do. But when I get back into the real world, it's so easy to forget." My response is always the same, "This is the real world. Out there is the movie set where everyone is acting."

In spite of what the dictionary may say about vulnerability as weakness, vulnerability is nothing more than speaking the truth. You may be embarrassed, ashamed or even scared of it, but it's still your truth. And until it's spoken aloud, until it's shared, it's a truth you hide *from yourself.*

The tough guy who's never afraid is more likely always afraid. The kid who never cries probably wants to cry all the time. The inspirational leader who can only talk about one subject is probably choosing to not talk about something that matters more. Everyone has something they're ashamed, embarrassed, angry, or sad about. This is what makes us vulnerable and makes us human.

Remember Harry Potter's invisibility cloak? He uses it to hide from the bad guys. Well, people wear virtual invisibility cloaks every day of their lives—and these disguises keep them from being honest with the people who matter the most (including themselves).

It's not that they want to hide from each other, or themselves. But when we see ourselves as powerless, when we see ourselves as "the bad guy," it's like we think we're doing the world a favour. Who wants to be burdened with the knowledge of the *real me?* But what seems wise and protective is really destructive. When we hide our emotions under a mask of false invulnerability, we are acting instead of living.

Being vulnerable means expressing what our heart feels, whether it's due to a difficult past situation or a perceived lack of something in our present life. As the twisted internal battle rages on, we yearn to be accepted even as we hide who we really are. In Carrie's case, she held an immense amount of shame around her past actions as a bully. While she needed to speak vulnerably about her actions, and she *needed* to get *real* and stop acting like everything was under control when she knew it was not, she was unable to bridge the divide on her own.

The one certainty in Carrie's life was every room she spoke to would include bullies, bystanders, and the bullied. By acknowledging her own role in that unholy triangle, she allowed others to speak the truth as well. The end result was the kind of shared understanding that moved everyone to a better place.

HONOURING YOUR SOUL

As is always the case when people have a positive experience with vulnerability, Carrie's story continues. At the time that Carrie learned how her willingness to be honest about having bullied others could prompt a new understanding of other problem areas in her life, she and her husband were living in a small town surrounded by unhealthy family drama.

They started to be honest about their own role in the drama, and decided they wanted out. Unfortunately, a move was counter-balanced by the economic reality of a retention bonus. Designed to attract and keep employees in the area, it had been paid up front. Carrie and her husband would have had to repay the money had they chosen to resettle before the contract ended.

Although tied to the bonus, the couple wanted out of the community. They saw the move as a chance to put some distance between them and the disruptive squabbles taking place amongst members of their large family. What Carrie didn't realize was that her own happiness was the true cost of honouring that contract. While she dreamed of moving to a city that inspired her, where she could help more people and not be distracted by family issues, she felt powerless to make the change. The longer she stayed in the hated town, the longer she postponed her speaking dream.

While there's always a cost to our actions, Carrie's choices show how we're not always willing to be honest (vulnerable in the face of our own truth!) about the real cost. When we move or stay in a place for monetary reasons we eventually pay a price for it. The social invoice will eventually arrive in the post one day.

To her credit, Carrie and her husband moved soon after the conditions of the retention bonus were released. Although they delayed the move, she's now honouring her soul and experiencing more fulfillment and happiness as a result. At the time of writing, I'm pleased to say Carrie is continuing with her talks and exploring a new avenue of delivering retreats.

THOSE BASTARD DUCKS

Carrie's willingness to stay mired in a bad situation is not unusual. I often hear people say things like, "When I get my ducks in a row, I will [blankety-blank-blank.]" The one thing I know about this kind of duck is that they never line up, and one will move just as your about to pull the trigger.

One of the greatest gifts Carrie might have ever given the world was a result of not waiting for all her ducks to be in a row. I urge you to take action without waiting for "the right" or "a better" time. Just do the thing you're dreaming of and see the difference you'll make in the world.

> *"In the absence of clarity, take action!"*
> *~ Philip McKernan*

CHAPTER 10:

A TALE OF TWO BUCKETS

"Happiness is more about who you spend your time with,
as opposed to how you spend your money."
~ Philip McKernan

PUTTING IN THE WORK

Have you ever picked up an old journal or diary and been shocked by this former version of yourself? Were you impressed by who you used to be (or pretended to be)? Were you stunned how much you've changed?

In the last chapter we spoke about vulnerability, and its transformative power. In this chapter, we'll be able to see an example of change in action and learn how self-work is essential to reaping the rewards of transformative change that we can use for ourselves, and ultimately, the broader world. While vulnerability without internal growth holds us back, diligent, authentic self-work transforms us from within.

THE FIRST BUCKET LIST

I love seeing what happens when people choose to do the self-work that transforms their lives. In Mike's case, the progress was stunningly captured when he shared two "bucket lists" made at different points in his journey. Mike wrote the first list before he began the process of reconnecting with his soul. It read:

- Own a Porsche
- Own a Criss Craft boat
- Own a lake house in Michigan
- Be a millionaire
- Own a tropical island
- Go on an African safari
- Swim with dolphins
- Travel in space
- Parasail
- Skydive
- Bungee Jump
- Ride in a hot air balloon
- See Northern Lights (Alaska or Iceland)
- Own a condo in Hawaii
- Direct 1 movie I'm proud of
- Fly a wind-glider
- Learn to play guitar
- Learn Spanish
- Learn to surf

Mike showed me this list, after which he and I shared a good laugh when he told me his true feelings about most of the items on this list. There were a few items he still thought worthy of pursuit, but the most incongruent items on the list were all of those related to adrenaline-inducing activities. "I hate heights. I mean, I literally shake when I'm in high places. I don't know what I was thinking when I wrote all of these things," said Mike.

We can all share a good chuckle at Mike's expense. But let's be serious. A list like this is not a phenomenon unique to Mike. There are some circles in which you could be written off as a pathetic loser if you didn't have an extensive bucket list. Those same people would also think that bucket list should include big, fancy items that would sound impressive when sharing the details with what I call your "bucket list buddies."

Hey, Richard Branson likes space travel and skydiving, right? Everyone wants to be just like Richard Branson, don't they? I'd make a hefty bet that if you looked at the bucket lists of 100 people, you'd see the same few Richard-Branson-like items pop up over and over again. You might find a Porsche instead of a Ferrari or a Hawaiian condo instead of one in Mexico. But the principles remain.

In other words, these bucket lists aren't really written for the people who claim them. They're wish lists for the generic person their authors think *they'd* like to be. Many people who have lists like this have no idea that the lists represent—and reflect—a desperate and disconnected state of mind.

Mike wrote his second bucket list after a couple of years of authentic self-work that focused on his own inner world. I'd like to stress the fact that he *didn't* look at his original bucket list before he wrote his second one. This is an important point because Mike didn't set out to write a drastically different bucket list. In fact, Mike was so disconnected from what was on that first list he didn't even remember what it said. It was only after he wrote the second one that Mike looked for his original bucket list in his old files. The difference is stunning. That second list reads:

- Stop trying to change others
- Stop living in the past, today is all that's guaranteed

- Stop living for the future and saying things like, "I'll be happy when . . ."
- Stop looking for answers outside myself and trust my intuition more
- Be inspired everyday by something (and hopefully inspire others)
- Stop thinking about money so much
- Be a proud husband and father
- Accept my family and friend's love for me
- Look in the mirror every day and love myself unconditionally
- Give up attachment to "stuff"
- Realize that life is the destination and the journey is the reward
- Embrace my creativity and spend more time creating, and less time "working"
- Spend more time relaxing with family
- Vacation more with family
- Start an art foundation for underprivileged children
- See my children marry their soul mates
- Get re-married on the beach where I proposed to my wife
- Have my second honeymoon in Hawaii and visit all the islands
- Drive across country in a VW by myself —has to be a VW

You might notice that this second list is a whole lot simpler. Can you imagine the pressure one might feel while trying to live up to the first bucket list? There's almost nothing on that list that isn't related to money—either making more, the status of having it, or spending it on items that confer status.

You might also notice that the second list is heart-centred. Within a couple of years of looking within, rather than looking for money and status, Mike's focus changed from financial greed (business success was solely based on making more money) to allowing

Mike to be the kind of person who makes a real difference in the world. His focus went from self-aggrandizement to meaning.

Can you imagine a world full of people acting from the heart and doing things in the way Mike stated in his second bucket list? This would be a different kind of world; one of compassion, love, and happiness.

This might sound gooey to you, but the truth is that these are the characteristics the world needs. We tend to try thinking on a grandiose scale about improving the world. The truth is that the best way to improve the world is by starting from within. This leads people to think in terms of contribution versus confiscation. Instead of "having" life, we contribute to it via our own family and causes we believe in. When we give instead of take, we find peace of mind. Too simple? Not at all. I've seen it over and over. Underneath it all, people just want peace of mind.

Once a year I run a retreat called Give & Grow where I take a small group of people to a foreign land like Guatemala. There we spend time in an orphanage just giving ourselves unconditionally. We then take space in nature hiking for a few days to allow the experience to percolate, and further process through conversations and questioning.

To see the peace in the faces of the participants is extraordinary and they report a contentment that many have never experienced. In our ability to give, lies our greatest opportunity to grow.

The good news is that peace of mind is achievable. The even better news is that peace of mind is the most essential ingredient to living a fulfilled life.

BEING HUMAN

Mike's long journey from the first to the second bucket list is another incredible tale of a man brave enough to travel the arduous journey to authenticity.

You see, just like so many of the other courageous individuals whose stories I've told here, Mike found through inner work that he wasn't living an authentic life. In spite of the fact that some people think authenticity is yesterday's news, I can assure you that there is still much to be done on the authenticity front. Yes, I have been told by industry insiders that authenticity has been "done." And I can also reassure you that line of thought is entirely inconsistent with my own experience as a life and business coach. More importantly, it's inconsistent with what I've seen happen to the people I work with! Indeed, I believe the quest to understand authenticity has barely begun, an opinion supported by the fact that so few people actually live an authentic life.

It's rare to meet a person like Mike who had the courage to dig into his story even before he realized he might have a problem. Let me explain. I met Mike at an event hosted by a mutual friend. At the time, Mike was quite certain he didn't need to change a thing in his life.

I was a guest speaker at the event and when Mike walked up to me after my presentation, his goal was to put me in touch with his cousin who, according to Mike, needed to "work on some things in his life." Mike assured me that he was fine. When I suggested we discuss this all later, I didn't indicate that I knew Mike's cousin wasn't the only one seeking change.

It's become rather easy for me to spot someone who needs to take their journey, and I saw it in Mike's eyes when I met him.

When we spoke on the phone, he expected me to ask about his cousin. Instead, I gently probed him with a few questions about himself. It didn't take him long to realize there were a few things in his own life that he needed to clean up. The next day, Mike registered for one of my programs and took the first steps on his own journey.

Mike is a creative and thinking man. In his own words, he was, "the kid with crayons in his hand and paint on his shirt." He followed his passion for creation by choosing art school over a traditional post-secondary degree. It took immense courage for Mike to do this in the face of pressure from family, friends, and society. On all sides, he consistently heard the same message: "There's no money in art."

Mike had a pre-existing condition that caused him to be susceptible to these words—he's human. Being human gives us access to a lot of wonderful experiences. But it often leaves us vulnerable to the words of others, especially when we're young and impressionable.

Being impressionable, Mike soon decided he'd be wise to take up something more practical than the creation of art. After his first year of art studies, he chose a major in advertising because, in his own words, "I thought it would be cool to work in advertising. All I knew was that everyone in the industry wore black and sat in cafes drinking expensive coffee all day long."

But I don't want you to think I'm just making fun of Mike. His experience is common in that we often make decisions about our life and our future based on what other people think. Is it any wonder his first bucket list was so extremely out of sync with his soul?

Now ask yourself how many people make bucket lists, either on paper or in their minds, as inauthentic as Mike's? If I was forced to guess on this matter, I'd say the majority of people walk around with goals that aren't their own because they follow similar processes to the one Mike did.

In fact, the indoctrination starts well before university because we start making choices that seem practical, but don't honour our soul, at a very young age. I do believe that people need a certain level of practicality in their lives. I, myself, worked in businesses and at jobs I wasn't passionate about during the period of time that I was making my way to the next stage of a more authentic life. Looking back, some might say I barely escaped practicality by the skin of my teeth! My point is that while we all need some notion of what's practical, we need to develop those notions while being authentic.

Many people miss that last step and live lives of regret. Having followed the standard path of buying a home and/or having children, they start to believe it's "too late" to get back on an authentic path. Often people cite a 'lack of clarity' as a reason to remain on autopilot.

In Mike's case, it's not as though he gave up on art the moment he declared a major in advertising. He'd arguably chosen a creative endeavour, and was able to learn much about art during his time at school, both in his classes and during his personal creative time.

After he completed his degree, Mike found some work in advertising. With his fascination for creation unappeased, Mike soon felt he had to do something about his passion for films. A committed movie lover who'd always been attracted to film, he applied for film school and was accepted there to complete a

Master's Degree in Film at a school in Ireland.

I didn't meet Mike until several years after he'd completed that master's degree.

Had I met him earlier, I suspect I'd have seen an interesting young man caught somewhat between the realms of practicality and passion. Stepping away from the practicalities of a good solid job in advertising to study film was courageous, likely more courageous than he knew at the time, or perhaps even now.

Upon finishing film school, Mike returned home to the U.S. and landed back in his hometown surrounded by his old friends. The move was challenging as Mike found it difficult to relate to the people he'd spent most of his time with. His life had taken such interesting turns—yet here he was, back where he started. Anyone who's found themselves in a similar situation likely recognizes how traumatic it can be.

The real issue is that we tend to think of these kinds of decisions as though they happen in a bubble, independent of the rest of the world around us. However, you cannot just move across the world, immerse yourself in the study of a creative endeavour, surround yourself with other like-minded people from around the world, and then roll back into your old life as though nothing has happened. After such an experience, you'll have changed, so going back is a tricky endeavour.

Going back is harder than leaving in the first place. What happens is that the person with the new experience changes so fundamentally by the experiences they've had that they'll either have to try to forget all the new things they learned or find a way to bring their new experiences back to the world they once inhabited.

Both of these paths are incredibly difficult. Since it's not possible to forget everything you've learned and experience, acting like you have is a sure path to disconnection and inauthenticity. Don't fool yourself, this path is more common than you might think. It's the rare individual who accepts the call to adventure to begin with, and those who do are often not able to re-integrate their new knowledge into the society they left.

After opening his mind to his passion in Ireland, Mike came back home and found that little had changed. He did, however, now feel like a stranger in the land where he should have felt most at home. It was in the company of his same old buddies where he felt his lack of connection the most.

While there wasn't anything wrong with his old buddies, they weren't good for Mike at this point in his life. As mentioned, he'd changed drastically, but the buddies were still playing out much the same script Mike had left behind. Sitting around drinking beer in the same old pubs and watching the same old sports teams on TV was now a painful exercise for Mike. It didn't take him long to see how far off their path he'd strayed.

But that was only part of the problem. Mike was also physically far away from the film school life he'd once lived. Like-minded friends from those days were scattered across the world, leaving Mike feeling very isolated.

Every day that passed back in his hometown, Mike lost a little bit more of the peace of mind he'd experienced in film school. New attempts to re-integrate him into his former life were complicated by the fact that he'd left that life, intellectually and emotionally, far behind.

This kind of dichotomy can tear us apart. Before he knew what had happened, Mike was in the throes of a deep depression. He felt hopeless, fatigued, and a deep sadness. At his core, Mike had never properly reconciled his passion with practicality. Even though he'd grown immeasurably during his film school foray, he was predestined to experience the struggle when he returned. He wanted a life of passion—and chastised himself for not being practical.

None of this was Mike's fault, but it complicated his journey back to his centre because it made self-work very difficult. Who wants to work on something we think is broken?

It would be dishonest to underplay the seriousness of Mike's depression. He was so low at one point that he found himself literally out on a ledge, ready to take his own life. Alone, forlorn, and exhausted, Mike eventually collapsed backwards onto the roof of the building on which he was standing.

THE ROAD BACK

It was a long journey back from the ledge and knowing that many would not have made it, it bears some discussion before I share more of Mike's story. The reality is that many people settle for what they have because they falsely assume they are not worthy of more, better or different.

While settling looks different to every person, most people who go on an adventure will later re-integrate into the life they left, often by taking a kind of middle path. This is normal, but it is also a form of settling. Finding the balance between this settled path and one's correct centre, requires true acts of courage.

For Mike, falling backwards off the ledge gave him an

extraordinary opportunity to make another search for who he wanted to be. A couple of weeks after his moment on the ledge, Mike met the woman who would eventually become his wife. That meeting made a big contribution to Mike's journey back, and it's no coincidence that meeting her provided an incentive to leave his hometown and take up his adventure again.

This idea that Mike would meet his wife at a moment when he was so low takes some people by surprise. But the phenomenon actually makes sense. You see, when Mike walked down off that ledge he was open, vulnerable. Important people, including future spouses, seem to show up in our lives when we're open to their arrival.

Without having the benefit of being there or knowing Mike at the time, I can still easily surmise how open he might have been at that time. I know what the pit of depression is like. I also know new ideas and modes of being are often born of dark places. While meeting the woman who'd eventually become his wife was a big deal, it was not the only event that led Mike back to his metaphorical centre.

On the contrary, as with many people who struggle with the passion-versus-practicality dilemma, Mike often felt himself pulled towards money. As part of that quest for money, Mike was working with some colleagues to put together a boutique ad agency. When a whale of a client fell into the young entrepreneurs' laps, Mike and his colleagues embarked on an epic kind of journey.

While he readily admits the youthful agency had no business landing an advertising client so big, the whale's arrival led to several years of hectic work trying to keep it fed. These were heady times. It was before the collapse of the U.S. real estate market and the pace was frenetic. The massive conglomerate that contracted Mike's company didn't know it was in the midst of an economic bubble and they spent advertising money as if the good times would never end.

Mike and his company made a lot of money during this period. Mike even says it was likely too much money. As so many young entrepreneurs do in similar situations, Mike found himself spending money faster than he made it. He was on a treadmill, and the conveyor belt was running at full speed.

We all know how the U.S. economic collapse played out. Mike and his colleagues were among those who got a rough ride. Mike's life was complicated by the fact that he now had a wife and kids. Interestingly enough, he was also starting to remember his passion.

While pieces of his passion for creation were not completely foreign to his work with the ad agency or other ventures Mike undertook in the years immediately following the wide-scale economic collapse, Mike really hadn't asked himself what his soul most wanted in a long time. Caught up in the day-to-day instability of working for money, he thought he was doing his "best," a state-of-mind that left little room to think about what he might like to be doing.

It was somewhere around then that I met him. The bubble had popped a couple of years earlier and Mike had put together some marketing opportunities that paid the bills.

It wasn't all bad, however. While he didn't yet know it, the skills and contacts he made would prove invaluable on his continued journey. More importantly, Mike's experience had engendered a kind of internal metamorphosis. The changes involved with that were bringing him to a point where he was ready to take the inward journey I could help with.

In retrospect, I feel lucky to have met Mike at just the right moment in his journey, and I am honoured he chose to share his journey with me. From that day forward, he hasn't shied away from asking himself the difficult questions. He has courageously moved forward on his journey, and he's seen remarkable results. That was made stunningly obvious in Mike's two bucket lists!

I'm not going to pretend that Mike's journey has been a big bed of roses. It hasn't. Like everyone who chooses to step firmly onto a path that takes so much work to master, Mike has had his ups and downs. But he never stopped asking himself the difficult questions. Nor has he wavered in his determination to make difficult decisions along his path.

When Mike started asking those questions, his biggest concerns were about what kind of a father and husband he was. Mike loved his kids and wife dearly, but he was concerned about his way of being with them.

He also knew stress compromised his ability to be the husband and father that he wanted to be. When he first started working towards his own truth, this was his most pressing concern. It was, of course, the issue he wanted to tackle first. But even though Mike was ready to do the work, he didn't see the connection between his family and relationship issues, and the fact that his work energy had been channelled into making money instead of pursuing his passion. Blind to this disconnect, Mike didn't see how taking time away from work could make him a better husband and father. Nor did he see how his first bucket list might be a counterproductive force in his life.

Once his eyes were opened to these facts, positive change came quickly. That doesn't mean Mike's work is done! In reality, transformations like Mike's never stop. This is natural. Once one accepts the challenge of stepping into the self-work and living the journey of life, they put themselves on a path of continual conversion.

And that's the road Mike is on. You've already seen his second bucket list, which is a remarkable document. While it's likely to change over time, it is a radical improvement over the first bucket list he created, and it clearly illustrates how far Mike's come on his journey. It's impossible to say what Mike's next bucket list will looks like. But I can say with a high degree of confidence that it's likely to be ever-more connected to who Mike is, and who he wants to be. As a result of that authenticity, it will be an increasingly powerful, beautiful, and effective tool to inform his growth.

Like Mike, most people want solid relationships with others. Even when we don't understand that as an actual life motivation, this connection between the internal game we play—and the external relationships these games create—is a force the authentic individual seeks to understand and master.

LET'S BRING IT HOME

Before you turn to the next section, please grab a journal and take some real time to answer these questions. Take your time on these.

1. Do you carry shame or regrets? List them and ask how they're holding you back.
2. Do you give too much of yourself to your kids or others?

3. What passion have you put aside in the pursuit of profits?
4. How much has/is money controlling your life?
5. If you had to give one last speech before you die, what would it be about?
6. What do you need to let go of in order to simplify your life?

PART THREE:
OTHERS

YOUR RELATIONSHIP TO WHOM YOU'RE AROUND

"Happiness is more about who you spend your time with as opposed to how you spend your money."
~ *Philip McKernan*

EXTERNAL RELATIONSHIPS

Often, I hear people refer to a breakdown in communication as the reason a relationship has grown apart or completely disintegrated. To ensure open communication, we're commonly encouraged to speak our *mind* within a relationship. Proponents of this "openness" believe it nurtures the connection between both parties. I couldn't disagree more.

But let me explain. I'm not against talking, and I'm certainly not against honesty. I also believe people in relationships must learn to speak from an intuitive place that I sometimes call heart, soul or even gut. But this inner place is not the same as speaking one's mind. My experience in working with people who are trying to do the self-work necessary to create authentic peace of mind, tells me the mind is like a computer. Operating in isolation, it acts upon internal logic, not intuition. This is evident when individuals voice their *opinions* as a way to go after what they think the mind wants.

This leads to confusion between thinking and feeling. In sum, I don't want to know what you think—but you can tell me how you feel all day long. It's how we *feel* about things that's our truth and people who bring that level of intuition to their relationship conversation will find themselves far more connected to those relationships.

A client called me from LA a few years back. As a result of not sharing his feelings, he was suffering in his most important external relationship. We began with me asking him about his life, his work, and the relationship with his wife. As we explored some of the challenges and frustrations he faced in his business and home life, it was apparent that he loved his wife. It was also obvious the relationship was not balanced, and that he felt he was compromising.

I asked him about his own parents and he told me they had separated many years ago. I asked if this would be something that he feared in his own marriage. "That is my greatest fear," he replied instantly.

"So how do you think that shows up in your marriage today?" I asked. After some silence he replied, "I bite my lip a lot and never say no to my wife, as I always want to keep the peace and keep her happy."

Despite pop-culture sayings like, "happy wife, happy life," it's not an individual's job to make someone else happy. Many of us try, but if you compromise who you are at the core, you compromise what you believe. The end result of that kind of effort to please someone else will lead to you building resentment towards them and yourself.

I urge you to consider all of your closest external relationships as you read the next section of the book. How are you communicating in your relationships? Are you sharing how you feel or what you think?

CHAPTER 11:

WAITING FOR LOVE

"It's more socially acceptable to be nice than tell the truth."
~ Philip McKernan

RELEASING EXPECTATIONS AND AVOIDING THE PAIN OF REGRET

Have you ever wanted to speak openly with another so badly that it was almost painful? In Part 2, we discussed several aspects of our self-relationship, which informs how we appear and behave in our external relationships. In this chapter, you'll see how internal awareness can inform our awareness of the potential pain of regret. You'll also see how it's our expectations that sometimes get in the way of improving external relationships.

Speaking our truth and expressing our love for another is important for strong external relationships. But it takes enormous courage to do so, and, I would argue, a high level of self-awareness first. The following story demonstrates how one brave man developed the courage to speak his truth and, in so doing, put an important external relationship on firm footing.

FORMING RELATIONSHIPS

Kevin is the youngest son of three in a family of farmers. He grew up as many farm boys do, working hard, playing hard, and having lots of fun.

Through the rough and tumble upbringing of a farm boy, Kevin grew into a gentle, kind, and friendly man. He speaks with the strength and determination of a man able to do anything. He also has a quiet presence, which is reassuring and endearing.

At times, Kevin can be humble to the point of insecurity. During my first meetings with him in my mentoring group, Kevin often referred to himself as "Just Kevin." This unconscious linguistic tic showed itself whenever he spoke of his pursuits and passions. Kevin qualified his words by saying "just" whenever speaking of his own pursuits. For example, "I *just* ran a marathon. I *just* got one new coaching client."

It was soon obvious that Kevin was on a path to improving himself in every respect. It was also apparent that Kevin was unaware that a number of relationships in his life needed attention. After self-reflection, Kevin did, however, recognize that his relationship with his father needed work.

He wasn't relating to his father, and through self-reflection, found the courage to admit this. That's important, because most people don't find the courage to deal with their parental relationships. They'll put it down to, "that's the way he is," or, "compared to my pal John, I have a great relationship with my Dad." We justify and settle in this way all the time, which is nothing more than a device to avoid facing psychological and emotional discomfort.

This type of relationship disconnect is common to many grown men, but Kevin had perhaps more angst about his relationship with this dad than most due to one important reason.

Kevin's two older brothers had chosen careers outside the farm, and were not interested in coming back. Kevin had seriously considered taking over the farm. To that end, he and his father worked together for several years.

Anyone from a farming family will have some idea of the emotions caught up in these particular intergenerational transfers. In many ways, the father's years of toil are seen as an investment in the dream of another generation working the same land.

For several years, Kevin worked at his professional job and spent evenings and weekends working on the farm. After years of torturous deliberation, he decided his life's path would diverge from the family farm. Although he kept some of the land that he'd bought, he knew he didn't want to spend his life there.

In truth, Kevin knew for years he didn't want to take over the farm. But since his brothers had bowed out of the business, Kevin felt like he was his dad's "last hope." Kevin never asked for that role, but he carried guilt and shame about the fact that he wouldn't live up to his dad's expectations.

To be clear, Kevin's dad is a hard-working man. You might even say he's a workaholic. Of course, there's nothing wrong with working hard, but show me a workaholic, and I'll show you a person running from something.

Kevin's dad is no different. His workaholic tendency was at least partially due to an alcohol problem he'd previously battled. Instead of healing himself fully, Kevin's dad turned his addiction to work.

As a child, it was difficult for Kevin to process the sight of his dad drinking himself into a stupor. When he quit drinking, it was welcomed by the family unreservedly. Turning to work was an accepted path, and he threw himself into work with the same drive that once led him to the bottle. This meant that for several years since Kevin was a child, his father had been working too hard.

As is the case for many farmers, they put their whole being into their farm, with heart, soul, and head all dedicated to the land and what it produces. They do this in the hope that their sons (sometimes daughters) will take over the farm.

Many farmers equate keeping the land in the family with their personal driving force, and this can lead them to put undue pressure on their kids.

The pressure can come from what's said as much as from what isn't said. That's because unspoken words lead us to speculate. In some cases, we invent expectations that didn't exist to begin with. This may have been the case with Kevin. He felt the pressure almost regardless of whether his father actually expressed it.

To make matters more complicated, it had been years since Kevin heard from his father the words he longed for in silence, "I love you." Kevin's psychological state about his dad was confused. In his mind, he connected the missing verbal expression of love with his perceived failings as a son. Kevin wanted his father to tell him that he loved him. But how was that even possible when Kevin was destined to break his dad's heart by not taking over the farm?

Through much self-work, Kevin became aware of this unconscious desire, and decided to do something about it. He went away by himself for a weekend to reflect on his relationship with his dad. While there, he wrote his dad a letter expressing his true feelings.

At the end of the weekend, Kevin drove to the farm and delivered the letter in person. After giving his dad a chance to read the letter, they sat at the kitchen table together. Kevin received what he'd wanted so much. His dad said the simple words, "I love you, son." But hearing those words was just the beginning.

Kevin's dad isn't a big talker, but what he did next spoke volumes to his son. Kevin's father folded the letter carefully, as though it was a rare scroll, and placed it in his shirt pocket. He then went to his room and retrieved a small box where he kept his most prized possessions. In the box was a locket he received from his grandfather, his father's wedding band, and some of the first love letters Kevin's mother and father sent to each other. Kevin had known about his dad's box of personal treasures for many years. Knowing the box contained items his dad treasured, Kevin was honoured to see his dad put his letter in the box.

Having received a gift he didn't even know he wanted, Kevin spent the evening with his dad before returning home to his own family the next day.

THE *REAL* LOVE LANGUAGES

Have you ever heard of *The Five Love Languages?* Written by Gary Chapman, the book explains that there are five different ways that every person experiences love. It also proposes that individuals are especially fluent in particular love languages, and then seek to express and receive love in that language.

For example, some perceive love through gifts. Have you ever noticed that some people are always giving gifts and others almost never give gifts? The love languages theory explains how gifts allow some people to express love. I think this is a valuable book in that it explains how different people give and receive love. It make sense that people express love in different ways, and this particular framework is helpful (albeit, not definitive).

The book suggests that knowing our partner's love language enables us to act in a way that's faithful to the partner's desires. The idea is that in the process, we'll improve our relationships. I find that problematic. Indeed, the more I thought about it, the less I aligned to the message. While I think the book offers several valuable insights, I was turned off by the rather robotic "prescriptive" nature of how the author encourages people to begin expressing their love.

In particular, I discount the idea that anyone should express their love un-authentically. As a coach and mentor who helps people understand their true inner selves, I believe a true application of a love language should honour how the *giver* likes to express love.

Let me explain. If we only try to do what we think our loved ones will like, our actions become mechanical and insincere. Eventually, that makes those expressions less effective—and less authentic. I respect that part of the process of developing an authentic way to express and receive love is to know that others show their love in their own way. Honouring and understanding this is a boon to relationships, and leads to much deeper connection and understanding.

When Kevin's father carefully folded the letter and eventually put it in a box with his *most prized possessions in the world*, Kevin finally understood that his father did love him, did not judge him, and did not hold a grudge for him not taking over the farm. Kevin's dad just expresses his love in non-verbal ways. Kevin realized his dad putting the letter in the special box meant showing his highest love to Kevin.

Kevin saw his father in a different light that day, and his lesson is relevant to all who want to allow ourselves be loved by others: we have to open ourselves to receiving love from others *without putting any conditions on how they express that love.*

Often we see an external circumstance we want to change. For example, Kevin wanted his dad to say the words, "I love you." He wanted his dad to come to him and tell him that he was loved. The ironic thing is that Kevin never told his Dad that he loved him, and yet he held onto to the expectation that his Dad would say these words to him. Kevin placed enormous expectations on this event, what it would look like, and how it would change his life. He thought he wanted the external circumstance to change. What he really wanted (because it's what he really *needed)*, was to understand his dad.

And what a gift that understanding was. Kevin could have told his dad that he really wanted him to say he loved Kevin, or he could have spent hours describing how much this lack of verbal expression has hurt him.

He could have done this hoping his dad would express his love and be more like Kevin wanted him to be. But even if he'd succeeded at that, the likely result would've been an unauthentic verbal expression of love from his dad.

It would have been as though his dad read *The* Five *Love Languages*, had the epiphany that Kevin needed to hear certain words, and robotically said, "I love you Kevin."

The gift that Kevin received was far more fulfilling. He learned that his dad loved him in his own way, and he received this gift after he expressed his love and gratitude to his dad *without* the expectation of receiving the same. You could say Kevin gave his dad the gift of his own (Kevin's) truth.

None of this means Kevin's family history wasn't hurtful or difficult. People often make the mistake of trying to sweep hurt under the rug. This isn't effective.

What's important is that Kevin gave himself an opportunity, when acting on his own truth, to grow and learn from his experience. He still wanted his dad to change his behaviours, and to live a more balanced life. But those desires affected Kevin less once he'd expanded his awareness of what his father valued in life.

In essence, Kevin learned to accept his dad's flaws as part of a larger package. He knew his father loved him and that he just expressed it in his own way.

Kevin's story beautifully illustrates that while we might not be able to predict the results of our actions or get exactly the result we hope for, acting from our soul's desire will always bring us closer to a more authentic expression of ourselves.

BEING OPEN TO THE GIFT YOU CAN'T YET SEE

Kevin has decent self-awareness, and this is probably what allowed him to see the true value in his father's actions. By placing Kevin's letter in such a special place, Kevin saw that his dad loved him, even if he expressed it in an unexpected way.

Breakthroughs like Kevin's can happen only when we are open to receiving unexpected results. I commend Kevin on being able to see the gift when it showed up, because not everyone does.

Efforts to re-ignite a relationship with a loved one often yields unexpected results. The instigators, who typically seek a particular result, often think they failed when it's not the result they get. Other times, the instigator thinks the other party isn't capable of certain actions. In either case, someone *fails*.

In reality, this perception of failure is based on the person's *attachment to a certain result*. If Kevin were attached to the result that initially spurred him to action (his dad becoming more verbally expressive), he'd have ended up disappointed, and unhappy. It's imperative to see each new development without attachment or expectations. Expectations are a trap. Release yours, take action, and embrace the gift that appears.

TAKING ACTION IN THE ABSENCE OF CLARITY

While Kevin received a wonderful gift in terms of his internal realization, the process that actually brought about the gift was based on his desire to change the external, and on the fact that Kevin then did something that *always* makes a positive change; he took action. And taking action is always the right thing to do.

I don't have a problem with reflection and discussion, but action gets results. Action brings change in your life more than anything else. Even those who take the wrong action come out ahead as long as they learn something. Even knowing what *not* to do the next time is valuable. At a minimum, you gain clarity from action.

When it comes to improving or healing relationships, the first action is often a conversation. Most people assume that conversation is with the other person you want to influence, but I think the best place to start is with one's self. A conversation with the other person *can* follow, but it's not always necessary.

This process of internal dialogue may take place via journaling, when you take space to be alone or anytime you find yourself in a space that conducive to an out-loud conversation. (I recommend avoiding Starbucks). However you approach the self-conversation, it's between you and you only. Only after the internal conversation happens do I suggest people have the external conversation with the other person. Skip this step at your peril—or ignore my advice and find yourself with a heap of regret over what you did or didn't say.

I say this because I know that people often wait for the right moment to speak to people about "important" topics. Regardless of whether you're trying to heal your connection to a long lost loved one, start or end a business, initiate a divorce, launch a new gym program, or start writing, there's no perfect moment. I also know that taking *some kind* of action begins the process of moving forward, whatever that looks like.

For example, Kevin knew he wanted a better relationship with his dad. He wanted his dad to tell him that he loved him. More importantly, he wanted to be honest with his dad about his own true feelings. Rather than find the right time to talk, Kevin conducted his own internal dialogue so he could be clear about his own position. In the end, it didn't matter that his action brought about a different result—because the real gift was stunning nevertheless. The fact that Kevin did not let a lack of clarity stop him from taking action is a powerful reminder of why it's so important to take action.

LIVING REGRET FREE

My wife, Pauline and I recently discussed her feelings about her father. She mentioned she had some unspoken emotions about her relationship with her dad.

I then suggested she write her father a letter to express her feelings. She thought it was a great idea, and that she'd probably do it one day. I then asked if she'd regret if her father died tomorrow and she hadn't written him the letter. She admitted that she would deeply regret it, then put down what she was doing and wrote the letter immediately. To her credit, she even sent the letter. Unsurprisingly, her actions were as richly rewarded as Kevin's had been albeit in a different way.

We often hear people say that we're apt to regret the things we *didn't* do more than the things we did. I think that's especially important to think about in terms of our close relationships and how the words we don't speak, and the actions we don't take, will affect us on our deathbeds, or when we sit, literally and figuratively, beside the deathbeds of others.

Why would we allow ourselves to live with regrets? Is the pain of taking the action or saying the words so difficult that we'll allow ourselves to live with regrets in order to avoid the pain of taking the action?

It's important to acknowledge that we are scared to say what's on our minds, and even more scared to speak what's in our hearts. Are we that scared to be vulnerable that we'll accept a lifetime of regret? Do we fear further rejection that keeps us from seeking acceptance?

I want to live a regret-free life. Since I doubt I'll ever regret not putting in more hours at the office, I spend more time with *my family and myself.* I take the same approach when saying what's in my heart. While I sometimes take heat for comments others deem inflammatory or counter-cultural, I don't regret saying them. It's not about speaking your mind, but rather speaking your truth.

Your truth comes from your soul and is a cleaner, unpolluted version of you. This kind of truth is an expectation-free being. In other words, the soul speaks truth, but the mind twists that truth by creating expectations that invent false-situations and paranoia.

When considering speaking openly and honestly to anyone (but especially a loved one) it is helpful to ask, "Will I regret *not* saying it?" This question gets at the heart of what really matters, now and later. For Pauline and for Kevin, the possible pain of regret spurred them into an action they had been avoiding. Best of all, this brought each of them closer to their own truth—and improved an external relationship at the same time.

"You will not be counting your dollars on your death bed
but rather the happiest days and moments of your life
and the people you shared them with."
~ Philip McKernan

CHAPTER 12:

TOY STORY

"Listen to your heart and then take action to honour your soul."
~ Philip McKernan

DEPRIVING OURSELVES

Have you ever wanted something deep in your soul, yet not allowed yourself the opportunity to experience what achieving that desire may bring?

It can be difficult to decipher the difference between an arbitrary desire and a soul's longing. (Remember Mike's wildly different bucket lists?) While it sounds counter-intuitive to the messages we often get from society, I'm here to tell you that people who practice purposeful selfishness can change the course of their own history—and transform personal relationships at the same time. Curious? Keep reading!

SEEKING A REASON

When John stepped into working with me he didn't know exactly why he thought this path was one he should be on. He knew he needed change in his life, but he only had a foggy notion of what that change might entail. With guided self-talk and some intense conversations with me, John learned he was waging internal war on himself on several fronts. His perceived shortcoming as a father set the backdrop for where he fought his biggest battle.

John provided some compelling reasons for his lack of self-belief on this front. He'd been working out of town for the past 16 years, and he felt guilty that his children, aged seven and five, had lived with an out-of-town dad their entire lives.

John is a high level consultant who works on large oil contracts. On some contracts he worked nine days on and five days off. On other contracts he worked seven on and four off. It was never the same for more than a year at a time, although John often took a significant break between contracts. In spite of this time at home, John felt disconnected from his kids, and that deep down, he was a poor father.

When we started working together, I questioned John about why he felt like such a poor father. He kept coming back to the fact that he often worked out of town and wasn't with his family every day. John wanted to change his work schedule so he could be closer to his family. He was convinced that would cure him of his lack of self-belief as a man, a husband and a father.

In reality, John was psychologically stuck between a rock and a hard place. On one hand he believed he needed to spend more time with his family. On the other, he believed he needed to keep his high-paying contracts in order to make enough money to support his family and please his wife. And money was an issue. John told me his wife was not willing to change her lifestyle, which was linked to income. Since taking a similar job in his hometown would mean taking a reduction in pay, John felt his options were limited.

John continued to work at his out-of-town job. Wanting to spend time with his family and sleep in his own bed every night, he faced a classic dilemma every day of his life. Deep down, John believed his only job was to provide money for his family. Unable to see any other value for himself, he tried to make peace with the idea that he wasn't sure he could handle any of the other roles fathers and husbands might have. John even went so far as to say his main value was money. Given that perspective, he was powerless to make changes in his life if it meant making less money.

While discussing the topic of taking care of ourselves during one session, John admitted that he had never bought himself something he liked. Because he'd previously stated that money was his entire world, everyone in the room assumed that this meant he was materialistic. In reality, John worked hard for money, but didn't enjoy the fruits of his labour in terms of enjoying nice things.

I found it interesting that John worked himself silly in a job he hated in order to make big money, but didn't splurge any of that money on himself. I asked if he could think of one nice thing he wanted, and in approximately 0.001 seconds he responded, "a Harley Davidson."

Often the speed someone answers a question is more telling than the actual answer. It's impossible to respond as fast as John did unless the answer is something that weighs heavily on the mind. John didn't have to think to answer my question. His response was already present.

Naturally, I took his immediate answer as an invitation to delve deeper into the issue. I asked him to describe what it might be like to have his Harley. Again, he answered automatically, and in an instant.

He then went on to describe a time he rented a Harley Davidson in Las Vegas and spent the day rambling throughout the deserts around the city. He and his wife were on vacation at the time and John described the feeling of bliss as he took off into the desert with the wind in his face. He described it as a meditational state, a feeling of total freedom accompanied by timelessness.

I hesitate to use this word, but the way John described the feeling he had that day sounded almost *spiritual*. It was obvious to everyone in the room that he *really* wanted a Harley Davidson. The only issue was that he hadn't given himself permission to buy the bike. Whenever I see someone deprive themselves of something in this manner, I know it's a matter of self-worth. To be clear: John could well afford the motorbike, yet deprived himself of it.

That day, I urged John to buy the Harley because I knew it would be significant action on his part. When I asked him what the hurdles were to purchasing the bike, he said that there were none, and that *even his wife* wanted him to get himself a motorbike.

Despite the fact that there were no *tangible* obstacles in John's way, he was visibly uncomfortable about the idea of spending money on himself. The biggest obstacle was a lack of self-worth. After much debate, John committed to getting himself a motorbike.

OVERCOMING THE HURDLE

And this is where John's story gets even more interesting. When

I next checked in with John (about two months later), he hadn't yet bought a bike. We discussed it further and John told me he still planned to get the bike. But every time he got close, he pulled away.

The psychological plot thickened when I spoke to another person in the group and learned John told that person, "I hope I get more out of this mentoring program than just buying a motorbike." What John failed to realize was what the motorbike represented. He was still seeking clarity—when action was what he really needed.

As it's not my job to tell people what they can't see for themselves, I stepped back and waited for an opportunity to reconnect with John. A month or so later, I heard John had purchased the motorcycle. I was elated. Wanting to hear the story of how it went down, I called him to discuss.

It turned out John had a specific motorcycle in mind. After some online shopping, John found the Harley Davidson of his dreams, but it was thousands of kilometres away in the state of Minnesota. John tossed the pros and cons around for a few days, then decided to go for it and purchase the motorcycle.

Still thinking this quest was all about a bike, John rented a trailer and headed towards Minnesota. He expected the trip to include a routine four days of driving, followed by writing one cheque. Unfortunately, John started feeling sick about one-quarter of the way there. In fact, he was so sick he had to stop driving to get a hotel room. Shaking with cold sweats, John lay crumpled up under the covers and resolved to turn around and go home.

After a night with little sleep, John woke up and reversed his decision. "I realized the sickness was one last battle with my inner demon." John's sickness disappeared after he made the decision to move forward. We never know where a breakthrough will happen. For John, it was in a nondescript little hotel room in the middle of nowhere. He was a new man when he drove towards Minnesota the next day.

Over the years I have worked with a number of people whose undiagnosed 'mystery illnesses' have disappeared once they faced their truth, and began living a more aligned life.

In fact, a recent medical study out of Carnegie Mellon University claims to have proven a link between stress and physical illness. But how many of us need more proof of this? Intuitively, there is an obvious link. John's sudden illness, and its immediate disappearance upon taking action, are a perfect example of the mind manifesting an illness. Let's not forget that John was the man who'd *never bought anything nice for himself.* Is it surprising his mind would create a last-minute reason to avoid spending the money on himself?

IT'S NOT ABOUT THE BIKE!

The problem with focusing on the surface level lesson is that it misses the real point. John purchased a motorcycle. On the surface, it seems a normal thing to do for someone like John with a good job and the love for beautiful motorcycles.

From the outside, John looks like another wealthy middle-aged man spending some money on an expensive toy. This kind of expenditure is almost a cliché of the "mid-life crisis" we hear so much about.

To call what John was going through a mid-life crisis wouldn't do justice to the depths of the emotions he'd been struggling with for more than 17 years. During that time, John felt his own value was in the money he provided his family. In his mind, denying his own truth was what he had to do so his wife and kids could have everything *they* wanted. Meanwhile, John deprived himself of things he wanted.

I'm not suggesting that spending money is always an answer to our problems. What I'm suggesting is that when we don't feel we deserve to feel good about ourselves, we will not allow ourselves the very things we want. John wanted the Harley so he would have a means and a reason to get out on his own and experience the freedom he didn't feel in day-to-day life. It wasn't about the Harley Davidson itself, it was about what it represented in terms of bliss and freedom. Depriving himself of the Harley meant telling himself (and the rest of the world) that he didn't deserve happiness.

Getting the Harley represented taking care of himself, something John wasn't accustomed to doing. This is where the internal battle raged. On one hand, John felt he was failing as a father (and therefore as a man). On the other, he struggled to put a value on himself. How is a man going to believe he's a good father when he doesn't value himself? Getting the Harley was one step towards starting to value himself.

I knew the Harley wasn't a cure-all for John, who would need to continue to develop in many other ways. But by getting the Harley, he took an important—and authentic—step towards treating himself with value.

MORE CHANGES FOLLOW

In the months that followed John's motorcycle purchase, several incredible things happened. First, he took to the road whenever he *had a chance* on his beautiful Harley Davidson. This was not a bike meant for the shop. John made up for all the years he'd deprived himself of his bike by going on trip after trip, which meant more and more time for the internal conversations that would help John improve external relationships.

All of that alone time helped shift John towards a more authentic life, and he made several more remarkable changes over the course of the next couple of years. With his self-worth now growing, John found time to integrate a fitness routine in his life. On the surface, he looks much healthier. But positive changes in his physical appearance are nothing compared to the vitality he exhibits in his daily life.

This is a phenomenon I've witnessed time and time again. As people develop a greater authentic self-worth, they begin taking greater care of their physical body. John was the perfect example of this phenomenon. It was stunning to see him transform physically each time I saw him after he purchased his bike. So much for getting "just a bike."

When I first met John, his sleep patterns and anxiety were an obvious casualty of his internal war with himself. He struggled mightily to get a good night's sleep. This played havoc in his life, and the lack of sleep compounded his stress.

However, not long after he started valuing himself by buying his motorcycle and exercising, his sleep pattern improved. Within several months, John reported having long, peaceful, and uninterrupted sleeps every night. This admission floored me, as I was so happy for John. Sleep is up there with water and air in terms of its importance to our healthy functioning in the world.

However, none of the shifts described above were as impressive as the shifts in his relationships, most notably the relationships with his wife and kids. First, John initiated a conversation with his wife about working closer to home. Remember that John believed she'd never accept him making less money, so this was a significant conversation for him. He told her he expected to make less money. Expecting a blow-up, he braced himself for her response. John's expectation was dead wrong. His wife didn't care how much money he made. She just wanted her husband home.

With his false belief about his wife's income expectation out of the way, John started improving his relationship with his kids. When I met him, John was certain he was a horrible father. However, as soon as he started spending a little bit more time with his kids, he realized his kids didn't see it that way. They looked up to him, and they loved him more than he had previously imagined was possible.

In a time of enormous change, this was one new realization that forced him to re-evaluate yet again. John decided that if his kids thought he was a good dad, there was no reason he couldn't start to believe it, too. John was seeing himself through his kids' eyes, and he liked what he saw. The cool Harley Davidson didn't hurt, but the core of their affection was all John wanted.

I knew John had made enormous progress when he told me one day that he *knew* he was an excellent father and that he *deserved* to be with his kids. That was a stunning shift from where John was at when we first met.

LIVING A LIE

John is an honest and decent man. Without even realizing

what he was doing, however, he developed a work schedule so he would be away from his family, thereby proving to himself what he already believed—that he was a bad father. This may be difficult to understand, but John's story is a great example of how people create situations, both positive and negative, to protect themselves. John's choices protected others from him (he was a "bad father" anyway)—and kept him from being honest with himself.

> *"We give ourselves what we feel we deserve."*
> ~ *Philip McKernan*

I asked John one day, "Did you ask your kids if they want all the toys, the big house, and for you to be away most of the time? Did you ask them if this was what they expected from you?"

It turned out he hadn't asked those questions. It also turned out they wanted their dad more than they wanted stuff. While I am very happy John found his way through the impasse, I know this phenomenon isn't limited to John and his family. People make wrong assumptions about what others want from them all the time.

For example, my wife often gets excited when she sees a doll or a little dress that she thinks would look beautiful on our daughter. "Oh my god, it's so cute, Maggie would look stunning in that," she says. Sometimes I ask, "Is this about Maggie, or you?" I'm not suggesting there's something wrong with buying your child a beautiful dress or toy, but we need to be real about what's driving it.

Parents often provide an excess of toys for their kids without realizing their purchases are driven by their own internal insecurities. In many ways we make sure our kids get more than we did as kids, even when it doesn't serve parent or child.

We believe if we give our kids what *they want* we'll be a better parent. However, what children want and what they need are often two completely different things. There are millions of children in the developed world that have every imaginable gadget, yet don't have connection with their parents.

THE POWER IN A STORY

John was shocked by the power of his emotions he held around being a bad father. Once he first started exploring this belief, he realized he'd carried that fear of fatherhood failure since before his kids were born. Think about that for a moment. *John thought he was a bad father before he even was a father.* This is the negative power of a belief.

The lead-up work to valuing himself (and feeling he deserved to be with his family) was about John getting in touch with his own story. This shouldn't surprise anyone, because our stories are hardwired within us. We frame our whole existence in terms of our story. This is why it's so important for us to discover our story.

In John's case, a big part of his story was that he grew up in poverty and was determined to ensure his kids did not. He shared a room with his brothers and wanted to make sure his kids had rooms of their own. Of course it's okay to want the things economic stability can provide for your kids. But since John's quest to provide clouded his own truth, it came at the expense of his connection to his children.

> *"Our past has created the present,*
> *and our present is creating our future."*
> ~ *Philip McKernan*

Remember when I said, "past is prologue," at the beginning of this book? Regardless of whether the individuals I work with think they're working on their relationships to self or others, an authentic understanding of their own story is essential to changing the trajectory of their lives. People who can't open those boxes are doomed to staying on the same path, without change.

Of course, many of us avoid opening our stories because the process can be painful. I know that. I also know that it's only a fraction of the pain that comes from living a life of regrets. Opening our stories means facing our current circumstances and our past, including poignant or painful moments. I have yet to meet someone who has dealt with them all, and that means we all have a story to explore.

Past hurts are *always* about relationships, internal or external. They're always about the way someone else victimized us, the way we feel about letting someone down or about the expectations we feel these relationships placed upon us. That's why our stories are *always* tied to relationships and the emotions generated when we feel we've wronged someone else, or been wronged ourselves. Once we get in touch with our own story, we can begin to change our feelings about the past. And this is critical. From changing our feelings, we can change our thoughts. From changing our thoughts, we can change our actions. When we change our actions, we are in control of our present. When we're in control of our present, we're in control of our future.

Facing his story, which really began long before John was married and a father, was an essential starting point for John. Taking action to value himself was his turning point. In this way, John's story is a heroic one. And anyone who thinks heroism has to involve saving a princess is missing the point. The changes John made transformed his family's life. In that way, John changed the world! The bottom line is that taking care of yourself, even when some might consider it "selfish," is an important first step in improving external relationships. In this story, we saw a man who didn't really understand the power of what he'd unleash. But once he embraced his own need for change, he could affect enormous change for others, too. Once again, the internal informs the external.

CHAPTER 13:

MR. GRUMPY

"The ultimate destination of fear is regret."
~ Philip McKernan

THE SPEED OF A DECISION

Have you ever laboured over a decision? Not knowing what to do is sometimes the result of the external labels others have given us. Other times, we use false labels to reinvent ourselves within external relationships. The end result is never authentic. Worse, false labels can hold us to a negative status quo.

In the last chapter, we saw how a man who learned to follow his intuition and soul's desire transformed his external relationships. In this chapter, we'll see trusting our gut sooner leads to faster results because it releases us from the internal (head) struggle and lets us follow our intuition instead.

A METAMORPHOSIS

A couple of years ago, a teddy bear of a man named Jack came to one of my retreats held in a beautiful and remote location. I choose venues like this so participants can focus on themselves with fewer distractions.

People often come to my retreats when they're at some kind of a crossroads in life. Some feel disconnected from particular aspects of life. Others struggle with external relationships. Jack was no different.

Then, as now, Jack is a successful man on paper. Working in senior management for a large corporation at the head office in Toronto, Jack made great money at his job and was doing quite well with his investments.

Jack also had a wife he loved dearly and two teenage daughters whom he and his wife had raised well. Jack was proud of his marriage, and of his daughters.

Before participants arrive at this particular retreat, we ask them to bring an object they feel represents them in some way. In the first session, everyone in the room introduces their object to the others, and explains why their object represents them. At that retreat, some people shared meaningful photos, or family heirlooms, while others shared objects.

When it came time for Jack to share his object, he reached into his backpack and pulled out a plastic figurine of a character known as Mr. Grumpy. If you know the *Mr. Men* book series, you'll know who Mr. Grumpy is. Each character in the series has one dominant characteristic, and Mr. Grumpy was, of course, known only for his grumpiness.

The sight of this large man pulling out a tiny plastic figurine prompted laughter from people in the room. The juxtaposition was amusing. Given the situation, there was also some tension and some of the laughter may have been in response to that. Regardless of what was behind the laughter, the gesture was vulnerable, and when the laughter died down, it became clear the object was not funny to Jack.

He explained how the figurine was a gag gift from his wife. She and their daughters thought the figurine was emblematic of Jack's grumpy demeanour. As a joke, they started calling him *Mr. Grumpy*. With emotion in his voice, Jack told the room he didn't want to be Mr. Grumpy any more.

The title was incongruent for me because I'd only known Jack as a big kind-hearted man. It was obvious that Jack cared deeply, and that he loved his family and wanted nothing but the happiness and success for them.

As the weekend continued, we got deeper into Jack's story, and it became apparent that Jack, like many in the corporate world, had gotten lost in his work. The lines between who he is and what he does were blurred. Like many men of a certain age and social stature, Jack had become obsessed with building a retirement nest egg to pass onto his kids.

In addition to working long hours at his job, Jack was also spending much of his free time building a portfolio of investments. As we dug deeper, it was apparent that Jack had spent his time on work and investments, but had *stopped doing personal things that make him happy*. No wonder he was irritable!

Once he was aware his problems were only a matter of degree (too much work and investing), Jack knew he wasn't too far off the right path. Indeed, the work and investments weren't even the problem. *He was just spending too much time on them and not enough on himself.* When done in the proper proportions, both the job and the investing could be just right for him and his family. Like so many people I meet around the world Jack had allowed his work to define him. When you become what you do, you have lost who you are.

Jack explained to the retreat participants that he hated being called Mr. Grumpy. He knew he could be quiet and sometimes brooding, but he didn't feel the label was totally deserved. He also admitted that his wife was somewhat of a socially dominant personality. Ergo, he felt somewhat railroaded into the Mr. Grumpy label.

On the final morning of the retreat, I was standing out by the ocean when I saw Jack walk by with something that looked a lot like the Mr. Grumpy figurine in his hand. Jack disappeared from view behind some rocks, after which I heard a splash and thought, "he didn't!"

When Jack walked past me back up to the room, I couldn't help but ask, "did you just . . ." He interjected, "yep, Mr. Grumpy is dead. I threw him in the ocean." The look on his face was priceless. He looked several years younger, and a whole lot happier.

The symbolic execution of the figurine was powerful, but what really mattered was Jack's decision to throw off the Mr. Grumpy label. He exhibited the power of a decision in that moment. You could tell that something changed for Jack over the course of the weekend. By actually disposing of Mr. Grumpy, Jack was making the decision to find his true self again.

WHEN A DECISION STICKS

There is a massive industry built around teaching people how to do things. "If you study how to optimize web content for maximum hits, you will find that putting the words "how-to" in your content's descriptions and tags will bring more views than if you leave them out. The logical reason is that people often type "how to . . ." into the internet search bar. People are obsessed with learning how-to do things.

The risks associated with the how-to culture came home for me the other day when I was on a webcast speaking about passion. The interviewer made the point that passion is a widely-used concept that's believed to be a great thing. He then said that most people are forced to live within the confines of certain external realities, and that if anyone was expected to follow their passion, especially to earn money from their passion, that they'd need to know how to do so.

His point was that it sounds almost magical to say, "follow your passion, and the money will follow." My interviewer wanted more than just magic pixie dust. He wanted me to explain *how* one follows one's passion. He wanted the *how-to* recipe for success. This is common—and misguided.

My point is that people often go to seminars to learn how to do this or that. They leave pumped up and excited to make change, but they don't always (or even usually) make change that lasts.

Some people leave retreats or seminars with a kind of residual energy, and they may use it make some temporary changes. But this focus on the '*how*' leaves few with enough steam to make permanent changes.

I believe that my clients' success in making permanent (authentic) change is rooted in the focus on *why* and *what* rather than how. My clients, because they do the inner self-work that gives them the courage to make the necessary change, have a remarkable record of making big changes—that stick. This doesn't surprise me. *How* has a way of showing up after we know *why* and *what*.

Here's the reality about *how*: there's almost no skill or strategy you can't learn for free by intelligent use of Google, YouTube, or a blog. Indeed, there's an overabundance of ways to learn *how* to do anything.

On the other hand, changing yourself from within, so you become the kind of person who makes change stick, cannot be learned from anywhere else but from within. Information isn't the key to unlocking this journey of life. You can be taught to take space, which cultivates self-knowledge. You can even work with someone who asks questions that promote self-reflection. But nobody else can change you from within.

When Jack left my retreat, he had that look about him like someone who'd made change stick. He didn't look fired up or excited. He looked like happy, grounded, and relaxed.

That's because Jack *embodied* the change he wanted to make. This is different than leaving a retreat pumped up to go home and implement all the changes we think we now need to make. By asking himself why and what questions, Jack cleared his persona of Mr. Grumpy. The reality of what that meant to Jack's life was evident about two years later when Jack's wife wrote me a letter to tell me how much Jack had changed and how fulfilled and happy he was. The change had stuck!

THE SPEED OF CHANGE

The notion that we can make a fundamental change in an instant can seem counter-intuitive. In reality, much work must be done in advance of the change itself, but the decision to make that change happen can occur in an instant.

Jack spent the entire four-day retreat digging into his story and exploring *why* he'd become Mr. Grumpy. He also thought about what he truly wanted from his life. In other words, Jack showed up ready to make change. All the retreat did was the catalyse that change in him.

Jack took the self-knowledge he gained at the retreat and used it to thrust himself towards change, and everything changed from there. I don't know when Jack's "moment" occurred, but if I had to guess I'd say it was when he woke up the morning of the last day and decided to throw that plastic figurine away, thus signalling a massive shift in how he would live his life.

Jack's story isn't unusual. When we're ready, we can change everything in an instant. I've had several such moments in my life, including one while living in Edmonton, Alberta, a few years ago.

I love the great people of Edmonton. But after living there for a year, I sincerely missed the year-round greenery that I'd grown up with in Ireland. Pauline and I had considered moving away from Edmonton when I had my moment of decision.

I was at the gym one morning when a lady came in and was working out beside me on one of the stationary bikes. As we chatted, I told her how I loved to run in the river valley, but that I didn't find winter running in Edmonton to be enjoyable since it was cold and slippery.

She then told me her solution to this problem. A few times per week, she'd meet her friends at the West Edmonton Mall (one of the world's largest shopping malls) where they'd power walk for an hour or more.

In that moment, I knew I was moving. There was no more "thinking about it," no more weighing the economic reasons to stay. It was just over.

I can't say what it was about this lady telling me her story that pushed me to be so certain of the resulting decision. Some might see her winter fitness strategy as a resourceful solution for getting exercise during the punishing Edmonton winter. But for me, it didn't fit. I went home from that conversation and said to Pauline, "I have to move. I cannot do this any longer."

Previous to this, we'd had long dialogues about our different options in terms of where we could move, what we'd do when we moved, and the pros and cons of continuing to own or rent the property we lived in.

We were stuck in limbo about many of the decisions we faced. But the day I told Pauline we had to move, her immediate reaction was, "okay." There was no second-guessing, no pros, and no cons. Once I knew, she also knew. In reality, the gym conversation was a catalyst for a move that had been percolating in me for a long while. Until then, however, I wasn't listening to my intuition—even though it was screaming at me to leave.

HEART OVER HEAD

My Edmonton tale reveals an important concept I've learned in the 10 years I've been coaching couples. I find couples are often confused when I tell them, "100% of couples I've worked with want exactly the same thing."

This statement doesn't mean each person in the couple doesn't sometimes feel like we want completely opposite things. As one attendee finally surmised, "we want the same thing, but we're speaking a different language."

In my ebook, *Dead Man Walking*, I talk about the power of getting out of your head and living from what I call your soulset rather than your mindset. This comes from personal experience. Prior to listening to my intuition that day in Edmonton, I was unable to connect fully with what I truly wanted. I was stuck in mindset rather than soulset.

When the shift to soulset finally happened for me, it happened at the level of feeling versus intellectual thought. The feeling vibrated in every cell of my being. So I didn't go home and try and explain or convince my wife. I simply told her how I felt (not thought)

> *"Tell me what's on your mind and I will hear you.*
> *Tell me how you feel and I will know you."*
> *~ Philip McKernan*

The speed of my decision that day was as quick as it was for Jack to decide he was done with being Mr. Grumpy. The lead-up stages to the decision might have taken a while, but the decision was instantaneous. This leads us to an interesting question: can an authentic decision be pushed or does it just come when it's ready?

Based on the experiences of my retreats and programs, I know it's impossible to know how much work will have to be done before a person can make the kind of instant decision that sets their life on an authentic path. What makes someone ready for change is highly dependent on many factors, all of which emanate from the individual's internal experience. Nothing external can stop a person who's made an authentic decision. How could it? The excuses and justifications disappear when a real decision is made.

Looking at Jack's situation, few would doubt he could have left the retreat and fallen back into his previous traps. He could have continued to justify his right to be grumpy. He was, after all, busy with work, and always had much to do.

Once Jack knew *why* he'd been acting a certain way and why people he loved might see that as ever-grumpy, he was also able to see *what* he wanted his life to look like going forward. There was a confluence of critical information, feeling, and self-knowledge—all of which contributed to the major decision he made that day.

I'm always grateful and honoured when people credit me with helping them move their lives in a positive direction. To some degree, this is what Jack's wife was doing when she contacted me. While I appreciated her sentiment, it's very important to note that Jacks' own personal courage is what really fuelled his transformation. If Jack is looking for someone to credit with the changes he's made in his life, he need look no further than the mirror!

In sum, courage is unlocked by our self-worth, and our worth expands first with self-knowledge, followed by an acceptance of that self. We must accept who we are before we have any chance to become the person we truly want to be.

For Jack, that required a decision to trust his intuition. Once he could do that, it was relatively easy for him to radically—and positively—transform his external relationships.

CHAPTER 14:

THE SOCCER PLAYER

"A true friendship is one where you share
both philosophies and vulnerabilities."
~ Philip McKernan

LIVING LIFE FOR ANOTHER

Have you ever found yourself doing something that in retrospect felt like it was done for someone else's benefit? Would you believe me if I said people sometimes live their entire lives for their imagined benefit of another person? I've seen people do just that—sometimes hanging on to the other person's ideal after that person has passed away.

In this chapter, you'll see how an essential misunderstanding of one external relationship informed an entire lifetime of action based on attaining the kind of acceptance that could never bring personal satisfaction, let alone peace and contentment.

PLAYING FOR PASSION?

My Irish friends and family are going to make fun of me for

referring to the Beautiful Game as soccer rather than football. But since most of the readers of this book will be in North America, I will commit this sin for the greater good and clarity.

I want to introduce you to the story of a young soccer player named Kasey. She attended one of my weekend workshops a number of years ago. On the first day, we spoke about one of my favourite topics, passion. I spoke about passion and its relationship to work. Just as we were about to start doing some exercises on the topic, Kasey put up her hand and said, "yeah Philip, passion is great. But I've just spent the past 10 years living my passion, and today I have $400 in my bank account and I'm miserable. Following my passion has left me broke and unhappy."

"What passion?" I asked. She went on to explain that she played soccer and in fact played in the World Cup for Canada. The other attendees were taken aback by her statement. When Kasey exposed her vulnerabilities in relation to soccer, I knew the day was perched on the edge of providing a magical experience. We'd only just started the weekend workshop, and nothing brings a room of people together faster than vulnerability.

"Where is soccer now in your life?" I asked. "Nowhere," she replied. At that moment my intuition spoke to me and I reached into my bag and grabbed a book I'd recently been reading called, *Open: An Autobiography*, by Andre Agassi. I read aloud a passage that had stuck with me. That passage, written on the eve of the professional tennis player's last U.S. Open, talked about Agassi's growing disconnect from his sport. The paragraph I read ended by saying, "I play tennis for a living, even though I hate tennis, hate it with a dark and secret passion, and always have."

I barely finished the quote before another of the attendees jumped in and said, "hey Philip, that's not a very good example.

Andre Agassi retired from tennis with several million dollars in the bank and a safe and comfortable life set up for himself."

That person's statement reflected the entire room's discomfort with what Kasey had said and how I was encouraging her to continue. This did not surprise me. People tend to be kind, and Kasey's raw vulnerability prompted everyone in that room to go into what I call "solution mode." As Kasey had previously mentioned that she was interested in carpentry, people in the room were offering business ideas and strategies for her for carpentry, and even for soccer. They saw her vulnerability as weakness—and were trying to "help her through" the problem.

I said, "guys, the strategies are great, and there may be a place for some of them. But let's stick with Kasey's story for a bit." I knew that the real gold in this moment was in Kasey's story. I also suspected there was a disconnect between the story she'd been telling people (and herself) for years.

To get at that issue, I asked her what she was thinking about when she talked about carpentry. She told me her dad had been a carpenter as long as she could remember, and that he never made much money. In her opinion he'd lived poor. Kasey loved the idea of being a carpenter, but was certain that carpentry was the reason for her dad's poverty.

This was interesting information. Next, I asked her about her relationship with her dad. She responded, "It's good now." I latched onto that last word "now," and asked what she meant by that.

Kasey told me her dad had joined an investment club because he'd wanted to learn about real estate. Because she joined, too, she thought she had lots in common with him. Now that they had lots to talk about, their relationship was going well.

Taking a leap of faith that in the story behind the story I thought I was hearing, I asked her, "When you went all the way to the pinnacle of your soccer career, walked onto that pitch at the World Cup and gave every last drop of your being for your team and country, did your dad say the one thing you've always wanted him to say? Did he say he loved you or that he was proud of you?" My question was based on my intuition alone. I *felt* her lack of recognition from her dad was the root problem.

Kasey's head dropped and she went silent as the whole room waited to see what she'd say next. Finally, she raised her head as the tears rolled down her sad, angry face. "No", she said. She paused, then added, "I fucking hate soccer. It took me away from my relationship with my dad, which was the one thing I always wanted."

Once she stopped crying, we continued to talk. It turned out that she'd grown up in her dad's workshop. She loved spending time with him, and also loved the work involved in carpentry.

Kasey worked through several interesting internal conflicts during that weekend. The one thing she was certain of at the end of that seminar was that she hated soccer, and that it wasn't her passion.

The sad reality is she spent 10 years pursuing soccer excellence because she believed it would bring her closer to her dad. In reality, it pushed them farther apart. Agassi's comments show Kasey's story is not unique. Indeed, tennis great Serena Williams has said she never liked sports and doesn't understand how she became an athlete.

Kasey's story is a good example of how parents often push their children in a certain direction—regardless of what the child wants. This seems especially common in high-level sports, where athletic success seems to give parents a chance to live vicariously through their children the life they would have liked for themselves.

Remember, parental pressure is expressed through words and actions. What's unsaid is as important as what is said. Not that what's said doesn't matter. Agassi's father said if he had the chance to do it all again, he would not let Andre play tennis. Instead, he'd push his son into baseball or golf—because those athletes play longer and for more money. (Sometimes the truth really is stranger than fiction!)

The people at my retreats and seminars know I value authentic inner truths. Indeed, I believe that if the entire world took a truth pill which made us speak the truth even for one day we would have millions of politicians, athletes, movie stars, models, doctors, dentists, surgeons, and others tell the truth of their relationships to what they do.

Just because someone is good at something does not mean they will love it. Tiger Woods is good at golf. But has his success on the fairway translated into success at the most personal level? Similarly, pushing our youth to pursue academic strengths can lead them to take on careers that in the long run, trap them.

PASSION VERSUS EXCITEMENT

Many people reject following their passion because it doesn't appear sexy or cool enough. They think a passion should be something that makes us famous or great in the eyes of others.

When the things that make us happy come from a place of quiet and unassuming inner truth, we quash their pursuit as unworthy of our time and attention.

We do this because we are confused by the difference between passion and excitement. At its core, passion might more accurately be understood as our "soul's longing." We are, in essence, passionate about what our soul longs to do. Confusion over the difference between passion and excitement is at the root of my biggest issue with certain entrepreneurial communities, including those involved with real estate investment.

Don't confuse my message: I do believe real estate is a great asset class. To this day, Pauline and I are invested in real estate. But we are not passionate about it; it's simply one of the things we do, not one of the things we love. Far too many people confuse the two.

For example, I regularly hear people say they want to pursue a particular money-making scheme (be in cash-flowing real estate, working seven days a week or forgoing holidays) so they can eventually give up their jobs. That's when they'll do something they really love; that is: their passion.

But putting one's passion on the shelf, or confusing it with what you do to pay bills, is a soul-sucking endeavour. These people have souls that long to pursue passion. Unable (or unwilling) to do the work necessary to reveal what that authentic passion might be, they write vision statements and goals that are all about excitement. Few realize that "excitement" is often another way to say "big money".

I believe this comes down to our intense fear about not being as good as others. When we are afraid to be poor, afraid to struggle through retirement, afraid to value today over tomorrow, it's relatively easy for us to drop everything to pursue wealth ahead of real passion. In Kasey's case, the desire to be cool, smart, and great, allowed her to discount the greatness in smaller, more meaningful activities, including the skill it takes to build a useful object from wood.

The simple truth of the matter is that many passions have an element of mastery that doesn't always include a massive external reward like money or fame. But if we stay focused on the external rewards to every action we take, it can be difficult to see our own passion as valuable and desirable.

When we see our core passion as something with little or no monetary value, we'll naturally assume we're less than others who seem to have it all figured out. We begin to think we're not good enough or even broken.

This makes it easy for us to attach ourselves to unauthentic goals—especially the kind with easy-to-read-price tags. These goals often include the chance to participate in "club-like" gatherings, where joiners become part of the "in" crowd, be it university alumni, a professional organization or those who claim to share an investment "passion."

Without realizing it, those who pursue excitement versus passion adopt quickly to become characters in the movie of their own lives. Worse yet, they then compete for parts they don't really want.

You might be thinking, "screw you Philip, I really am passionate about this kind of work. How do you think you know these things about me?" Well, I know because I've been there. I grew up in a family of high achievers, and my brothers and I competed in everything we did. I always had a chip on my shoulder about looking and being good. When my brother David started Java Republic, the company which subsequently became Ireland's second-largest coffee company, I wasn't happy running and maintaining that business alongside him. I was an important member of the team, but I still felt I wasn't enough.

I now see how that sense of "not enough" led me to seek the excitement of what real estate appeared to offer. Over time, I've learned to understand my story and my drives. I now know how unauthentic it was for me to invest in real estate. I know it was all about looking good to others. It was sexy and cool to pursue wealth. To some extent, it was also about competing with my brother (who still owns Java Republic).

What I couldn't reconcile within myself was the internal voice whispering that I needed to help people. Back then, I didn't even consider my passion a viable business. Like so many of my clients, the one thing I was most "certain of" is that I didn't want to end up poor or even average in wealth.

Driven by an unauthentic view of who I was and wanted to be, I took this entrepreneurial ego trip to another level. I wasn't content to be a business owner, and a wealthy real estate investor. I wanted to be an *international investor*, which sounds even sexier. Before long, I purchased properties in six different countries.

Just like anyone else who ignores their true calling—and makes it worse by confusing passion and excitement—there was a cost. I woke up every morning with a knot in my stomach. And I knew that feeling all too well as it was similar to the knot I had in my stomach as a child when I was faking my way through private school. Sure that I wasn't enough, I wore masks, and I pretended to be someone I wasn't.

Comprised of pure anxiety, those knots were the direct result of doing what I was not meant to do. I felt anxiety when I faked my way past people who could read, when I faked my way into a position as a coffee mogul, and when I faked how much I liked being an international real estate investor.

What made feeling bad so horrid is the fact I remembered what it was like to feel great. That's how I felt during the summers of my youth when I'd roam freely around County Clare on the West Coast of Ireland. Today, it remains my favourite place on earth and the place I go to create space in my life. It's in this place I get my inspiration, and no surprise the location of my Irish Retreat.

Fast forward past my own intuitive breakthrough and I can honestly say I haven't felt a consistent knot in my stomach for a long time. Moreover, I never feel the old knot when it comes to working with people in retreats or coaching programs. These activities just *feel* right. I don't *think* it's right; I *know* it's right because it *feels* right.

When approaching life (and work itself) as a process, we are able to put fear in its place because we know "failure" is never a permanent state of being. How could it be? There's no problem we can't tackle when we love what we're doing, and anxiety decreases when doing the work we were born to do.

But be forewarned. If we chase excitement over passion, we never get to know the feeling that comes from working within passion. On the contrary, working within our passion is deeply satisfying. Getting to that point demands a willingness to value passion over excitement. Your ego will hate it, but your soul will love it. Passion fulfills our soul's longing.

PASSION AND OUR STORY

The bottom line is that passion is always an essential part of the story we are *meant* to live. They may not be flashy, sexy, or even cool, but they are at the core of your soul's longing. Other people may be able to help you find them—but only you will be able to identify what your passion really is.

Only you can let what's inside emerge, and come to the surface. That's called self-awareness.

For example, Kasey's real passion (carpentry) was for a quiet, unassuming kind of work. She valued mastery and persistence, both of which are vital to becoming an excellent carpenter. Let's be honest. Jesus is probably the only carpenter who's really famous, and the chance of Kasey reaching fame or fortune from carpentry are limited. But that doesn't mean she can't make a great living from it; it also doesn't mean she can't begin and end her work day without a deep feeling of satisfaction.

And that's my point! Because the opportunity to be enriched by doing what you love brings a different kind of wealth that many people rarely experience. One can imagine carpentry as a valuable life's work. However, Kasey's mostly negative emotions about carpentry kept her from exploring her options, let alone diving in. But that said more about her self-doubt, and more about her lack of connection with her dad, than it did about carpentry itself.

It's very possible some of her carpentry-negative ideas came from her dad himself. Regardless, of the origin, Kasey was caught up in a false belief that led her to pursue soccer for the wrong reasons. No wonder she was scared to take her life in a different direction. Kasey was afraid she might spend another 10 years chasing the wrong thing.

My heart melted when Kasey told me she joined an investment club to try and build some common ground with her father. For Kasey, there was nothing authentic about this new pursuit. She thought she had to contort her own soul longing to win love from a parent.

What Kasey, and anyone else seeking passion, needs to understand is that the authentic answer always lies within. We have to get in touch with what our soul longs for; we have to clear away the obstacles that keep us from recognizing, and then pursuing, our true passion.

This means understanding our story. It also means finding a way to let go of what we're currently doing if it's not leading us on a true path. Emancipation, even if it's from ourselves, is a worthy goal!

NOW LET'S BRING IT HOME

<u>Before</u> you turn to the next section, please grab a journal and take some real time to answer these questions. Take your time on these.

1. What one relationship do you want to deepen?
2. Are you holding out to be loved in a particular way or can you be open to a person loving you in their way?
3. Do you have a label given by others that you don't like?
4. Who are you seeking approval from today?
5. What are you not saying in life?
6. How do you really feel about money and how has it shaped your decisions in life?

CHAPTER 15:

THE AUTHENTICITY CODE

"Fear is the assassin of dreams."
~ *Philip McKernan*

EXPLORING OUR GREATEST FEAR

I've said it before, and I'll say it again: our greatest fears have nothing to do with public speaking, darkness or spiders. We fear not being loved. Indeed, at certain times in our lives we may want to be loved so badly that we're willing to do whatever it takes to have those emotional needs met. We pursue careers and relationships as if they matter to that quest. And when we do that, we often step away from our truth because we think that's what it takes to make sure people accept us, to make sure people love us.

This quest for love manifests itself in a different way in every person. One of the saddest examples I have of that is personified by the story of a woman I know who hurts herself with poor eating habits and not exercising, yet won't change.

When I dug into her story, I learned this successful professional believed staying unhealthy was essential to maintaining a relationship with her mother. This version of the truth was fundamentally dangerous—and her fear of not being loved made it very difficult for her to give up. Remaining stuck in the status quo brought nothing but unhappiness and health problems, yet she chose to remain in that state versus face the alternative.

While that example seems extreme, the desire for love manifests itself in many harmful ways. Take another entrepreneur I coached who was estranged from his dad several years ago. He publicly declared his dislike for his father, and vowed never to speak to him again.

Professionally, this entrepreneur was driven to succeed and to be rich. He was driven so hard to be wealthy that he even neglected his family, and missed experiencing part of his own kids' youth.

But that was just the tip of his own proverbial heart iceberg. I learned two very important facts about this guy. First, his father was a wealthy businessman, and second, my client told his wife at the start of their marriage that he'd provide her with millions of dollars within five years of their wedding.

In spite of his claim that he'd never allow his father back into his life, the truth was that he so wanted to be loved by his dad that he'd spent his life emulating his father's version of success. Like his dad, this man was determined to be a big-shot businessman. Once that happened, he would be worthy of love.

This man's whole conception of love was based on performance and professional success, especially the accumulation of money. Even his promise to his wife was about performance. He wanted to perform for his wife; he wanted to perform for his dad. Instead of asking his wife what she wanted, or being honest about how his relationship with his dad was poisoning his life, this man assumed that making money was essential to being loved.

It's no surprise he neglected the most important elements of life. His health suffered, happiness was impossible, peace of mind wasn't even a consideration. And part of him didn't even mind. Prior to a major epiphany, he thought he'd rather be miserable than admit what he really wanted was to be loved, by the man he wanted to hate.

LIVING UN-AUTHENTICALLY

Love is essential, and we all need to live in love. We need to act from love in order to be happy and successful. Love fulfills us, love drives us to do wonderful things.

But there is a darker side to the pursuit of love because it can lead us to do self-destructive things when our quest is not authentic. Those confused by unauthentic love will lead unhealthy lives driven by addictions or unhealthy life strategies. They will neglect a chance at real happiness by acting as though performance matters more. They will pretend to value what they think other people want them to value; they will wear masks even though the masks make them miserable; they will stifle their inner voice because a louder voice tells them they are not good enough.

And what a tragedy that is! This book's title, *Rich on Paper, Poor on Life*, says more about poverty of spirit than it does financial wealth. My goal was to show, by example, what people risk when they give up what really matters—and what they get when they step onto a truer path. In sum, the pursuit of meaning, and peace of mind should never be exchanged for the meagre rewards of money and prestige.

WHY THE TRUTH MATTERS

The truth is that others love us when we truly become authentic, live the life we want at our core, and make no apologies for it. To become authentic, we must first start to love ourselves. Without self-love, and self-acceptance, we are not able to let people love us to the extent we need.

Most people arrive at my retreats and coaching programs ready for change. But few know what that change involves. At the core of this longing, they are sick of the false promises they've been sold about what happiness is supposed to look like. Some still hang onto the idea that wealth equals fulfillment—and is essential to everything from a happy family to a positive working environment. They soon learn why that quest is taking them in the wrong direction!

In sum, the only real way to end this search for wealth is to reorient yourself to what authentically matters in life. We all know in our core what's important, and it can be rediscovered by listening to our soul's longing.

We need to stop pursuing happiness and turn our attention to meaning. Happiness is simply a by-product of living a life that means something.

OUR RELATIONSHIP TO MONEY

Money is not the bad guy here. It's our relationship to money that's dysfunctional. We give money way too much respect, and place huge expectations on what it can deliver. We have given it power it simply does not have. We have put it on a pedestal it does not deserve.

In recent years, I have begun to explore our relationship to money and how that affects the trajectory of our lives. It's helpful to know that research shows money stimulates the same part of the brain as cocaine. Known as the ventral striatum, it's the part of the brain that gives you pleasure. The issue is that the kind of pleasure money (and cocaine) provides is experienced in bursts as opposed to sustained feelings. The temporary nature of pleasure makes it a form of "doing happy." (More meaningful fulfillment comes when we find ways of "being happy").

This was evident to me during a recent full-day workshop I ran, where money was the focus.

One highly successful entrepreneur told me, "money comes and goes and I have no emotional charge around it." Hours later, the same person dramatically changed her tune after tapping into her own immense disdain, and even anger, towards money. She admitted that she doesn't like to focus on or talk about money. All of this negative emotion was causing some real issues with her cash flow, but she didn't even know it.

Another business owner began the day by saying, "I have a good relationship with money, and I don't let it control me at all. It's just a tool." Later on, after exercises and discussions revealed the haunting truth of her own reality, she admitted that money had influenced every career decision she had ever made. This truth was startling, scary, and sad for her.

All of which brings me back to this book's central contention: authentic self-awareness helps people figure out who they really are, and who they want to be. Without that, people do not even have the knowledge they need to get real about why they do the things they do.

It's often suggested we all have a book in us. I believe we have two. The book we think will sell, and the book we know we have to write. This book is the latter. I hope it helps you find the courage to ask yourself tough-to-answer questions about who you really are and what you really want to do. Going forward, the answers will lighten your pack, and illuminate your path . . .

THE LAST WORD

"Your time is limited, so don't waste it living someone else's life.
Don't be trapped by dogma - which is living with the results of
other people's thinking. Don't let the noise of other's opinions
drown out your own inner voice.

And most important, have the courage to follow your heart
and intuition. They somehow already know what you truly
want to become. Everything else is secondary."

~ Steve Jobs

A NOTE FROM THE AUTHOR

I am in Ireland at the moment putting the finishing touches into
this work and trying too hard to stop the old thoughts driven by
the fear that this book is not good enough. That I am not good
enough. Those voices have diminished but not disappeared.

Each year I run a week long experience in a remote village on
Ireland's west coast. People fly in from all over the world to attend
this intimate event. I have often said I believe I get as much, if not
more, from the clients who come to me to better their lives. I take
great courage from the words of this poem written by a client
while in Ireland with me.

Always be Yourself

Listen to your heart, that's your true compass

Slow down, relax, be still, breathe

Get outside in nature - the trees, the wind, the grass, the birds

This is a voice that has no words

Quiet your mind, release your confinement

Trust your soul, your true alignment

Be grateful, be happy

For you always knew,

That this is the real magnificence of you.

~ Marie Osborne
(BraveSoul Ireland 2013)

*"If you want information go to Google.
If you want meaning come to me."*
~ Philip McKernan

To learn more about the author visit:
www.PhilipMcKernan.com

77364077R00142

Made in the USA
Columbia, SC
29 September 2017